CONTENTS

INTRODUCTION
by Thomas S. Szasz, MD

In an aphorism that is more attractive than accurate, Sir William Osler asserted: "A desire to take medicine is, perhaps, the greatest feature which distinguishes man from other animals." For our purposes, however, it would be more important to note that all animals ingest various substances, but only man *calls* some of these things drugs—or medicines or poisons—and then proceeds to promote or prohibit them.

Because people ingest and inject drugs—with and without medical advice, legally and illegally, to their benefit and detriment—we are presented with certain individual and social behaviors. The central question with respect to trying to *understand* these activities is: Why do certain persons and groups use (or avoid) this or that drug? And the central question with respect to trying to *control* them is: What should people do—through custom, religion, law, and medicine—to discourage (or encourage) the use (or avoidance) of this or that drug?

Because people also approve and disapprove, promote and

prohibit the use of various drugs, we are presented with another set of individual and social behaviors. The central question with respect to trying to *understand* these phenomena is: Why do certain persons or groups at certain times approve or disapprove, promote or prohibit this or that drug? And the central question with respect to trying to *control* these actions is: What should individuals and groups—through writing and teaching, lobbying and lawmaking—do to discourage or encourage certain social attitudes and policies with respect to drugs and drug users?

In short, why a person *uses* a drug is one thing; how others, or society, *react* to his drug taking is quite another. Accordingly, we are confronted with a choice between two fundamentally different problems and tasks: One is to study and influence the individuals and groups that use certain drugs; the other is to study and influence the individuals and groups—especially, the formally constituted authorities and agencies of social control—that judge and regulate the use of certain drugs.

It is the great merit of John Rublowsky's *The Stoned Age* that it deals as much with the reactions to drug use as with drug use itself. Actually, Rublowsky does more than present "A History of Drugs in America," as he promises in the subtitle, for much of what he says about the use of and reactions to drugs in the United States applies, with suitable modifications, to other cultures and countries as well. The historical materials he has assembled—especially about the use of alcohol and tobacco—are important and indispensable to anyone who wants to be seriously informed on this subject. Finally, his recommendation on how to deal with the problem, which I shall not give away here, is sound and simple. But it hinges on an assumption which he does not articulate or discuss—

namely, that the American people might yet prefer politicians who leave them alone to protect themselves from drugs to politicians who protect them from drugs by persecuting their fellow citizens as "addicts" and "pushers."

Indeed, we cannot have it both ways. Either our problem is the addict—an agent of malefaction infected with a dread malady—whom we must protect from the pusher and cure of his disease, or it is the politician—an agent of domination possessed with a passion for paternalism—against whom we, the citizens, must protect ourselves. I agree with John Rublowsky that the latter is, by far, the graver of the two dangers that now face us.

It is time—if it is indeed not too late—that we look more closely not only at what harmful drugs and profit-hungry pushers do to us, but also at what harmful laws and power-hungry politicians do to us. In the history of mankind, many more people have been injured and killed by laws than by drugs, by politicians than by pushers. We ignore this lesson at our own peril.

February 1, 1974   THOMAS S. SZASZ, MD

PREFACE

IATROGENIC is the curious term for illness created by doctors and their institutions, disease paradoxically caused by the very health agents whose function is to heal and prevent. Because it is largely a creation of our own misinformation and irrational fears, the American drug problem, a social malady of vast cost and distress, is an iatrogenic social illness. Like Frankenstein's monster, it has developed a life of its own that threatens us all. Frankenstein's monster was destroyed by fire. How do we cope with something as intangible as myth and as stubborn as collective delusion?

Strangely enough, most people today consider themselves well informed about drugs. At cocktail parties, a martini in one hand, a cigarette in the other, they discuss knowledgeably such matters as addicts committing slow suicide or speculate over the reasons why the terrible drug traffic can't be brought under control. In truth, virtually all that most people read in the press tends to obscure the facts. The rationale for this book's existence is that the drug problem cries for historical perspective and that understanding of the facts is the critical first step in alleviating what is perhaps the most intractable social problem of our age.

J. R.

13

1. ❖ PANIC

THERE is a panic in the streets that radiates out from our cities in widening circles that threaten to engulf the entire country. It is as though a new plague had been turned loose on the land. No one is safe. It strikes the rich and the poor; black and white; the city and the country. The specter of drug addiction—the fifth horseman of the Apocalypse—casts a shadow that darkens the lives of all Americans, everywhere.

To most of us, drug addiction appears to be a comparatively new problem, one that has mushroomed ominously in the past few years and, from all reports, is growing at an epidemic rate. One need only open a newspaper or magazine or tune in on a television news report to be reminded of the danger. Drugs in the cities; drugs on campus; drugs in the army; drugs in suburbia; drugs in rural communities; drugs in the high schools and junior high schools; drugs everywhere despite unprecedented efforts by federal and local authorities to stamp out the menace.

Even more sinister and frightening is the fact that this epidemic seems to be primarily an affliction of youth and early adulthood. It attacks the most vulnerable portion of the population. It is this factor, together with the novelty of drug addiction as a serious social problem, that makes the issue so emotional. Drug abuse appears to be a new element in the spectrum of ills besetting society, something that we did not have to worry about before. Drug addicts were slinky China-men and Levantines—NOT OUR CHILDREN!

The problem of drug addiction is thus charged with two emotion-triggering factors: (1) It is something that, at first glance, appears to be new and alien to the American experience and is seeped with all the suspicion and fear associated with the unknown; (2) it attacks our youth, and nothing arouses more emotion than that which affects our children.

It is not surprising, then, that no other issue affecting individual or public health and safety arouses the same degree of unanimity and zeal for reform and *revenge*—not juvenile delinquency or alcoholism, not smog or radioactive fallout, not inflation or unemployment, not smoking tobacco or pollution of our waters. Addiction is like sin: Everyone is against it except the addict . . . and those who profitably supply him . . . and, perhaps, those who are involved with the various federal, state, and local drug programs—*a $600,000,000 annual growth industry!*

Learned and distinguished judges, presiding over some of the highest courts in the land, have branded the illicit traffic in drugs our most terrible crime—worse than murder, rape, kidnapping, or armed robbery. One, Federal Judge J. Cullen Ganey of the Philadelphia District Court, voiced his regret that the highest penalty permissible was not heavier in sentencing a convicted seller of narcotics. He said:

This individual's crime rises higher in my estimation than that of any other I have ever had before me. . . . Anyone who can stoop to the low level of cunning to make a living by not only selling but supplying drugs to peddlers and others, I think, must stand the full weight of the law. . . . I am satisfied from his record that he is one of the persons who must pay the penalty, which I deem the lowest I know in the law, for indulging this offense. . . .

Federal Judge Phillip Forman, of the U.S. Court for the District of New Jersey, concurred in this opinion. In sentencing another convicted narcotics peddler, Judge Forman made this remarkable statement:

What you have done is like carrying diphtheria germs or smallpox germs into the community. Indeed, I think if I had a choice between the two evils, I would rather have a diphtheria epidemic or a smallpox epidemic than I would carriers of narcotics into the community because with diphtheria or smallpox we find out the source of the germ—it is either bad milk or bad water—and we can stamp out the source. We can vaccinate people and give them medicine. Some of them would be victims who would die, others would be cured, and we could clean the neighborhood out. But with carriers of this horrible germ, purveyors and peddlers of narcotics, we cannot get to the source . . . and we just have this germ going through the community from day to day. . . .

Although their choice of language in voicing these opinions may not have reflected judicial restraint, Judges Ganey and Forman undoubtedly reflected public opinion. Most people would agree with them, though they could not say precisely why. What is this crime that rises "higher than any other," that is worse than a "diphtheria epidemic" that would kill and hospitalize its victims?

In the emotion-charged atmosphere that envelops the question of drug addiction, it is difficult to arrive at a reasonable evaluation. Drugs have had an extraordinary impact on contemporary life in America. In one way or another they affect us all. No other social problem has generated so much debate and controversy and so few practical answers. No other area of public concern is so riddled with half-truths, myths, and patently false information.

Drugs, of course, are familiar to all of us. There are few people in America who have not used drugs of one kind or another sometime in their lives. Most drugs are considered beneficial. Indeed, we could not do without them. We take aspirin for headaches; barbiturates to help us sleep; Benzedrine to wake us up; tranquilizers to soothe our nerves; vitamin tablets to ward off colds; antihistamines to clear a stuffed nose. Some drugs, such as alcohol, nicotine, and caffein, are so common and are used so often that we do not think of them as drugs at all.

The drug problem, however, does not lie in these familiar preparations and nostrums. The problem is centered on *abuse* of what the federal and state laws define as "dangerous drugs." Included in this category are narcotics—literally, drugs that put you to sleep—both natural and synthetic, which are considered hard drugs; psychoactive substances like LSD, DMT, mescaline, peyote, psilocybin, and psilocin that alter one's state of consciousness; marijuana, which is erroneously included among narcotics though it is actually unlike any other drug in either its chemical structure or its effects; and, in the most recent compilation, amphetamines and barbiturates, plus cocaine, which is a powerful natural stimulant.

Most of the controversy surrounding our drug laws centers on precise definitions of the terms "abuse" and "dangerous." Of the two terms, "abuse" is the less difficult to deal with. In this context it simply means use of a drug (any drug) beyond medically prescribed necessity. The word "dangerous," however, is more slippery and defies adequate explanation or definition.

Some of the drugs listed in the "dangerous" classification are addicting—that is, the body develops a tolerance to them, and the user suffers withdrawal symptoms when the drug is not taken. Some cause direct organic and physiological damage. Some are believed to affect the brain and alter the state of mind to the extent that this alteration triggers criminal or antisocial behavior, causes mental deterioration, or leads to violence against oneself or others. Some have none of these properties, and to complicate matters further, there are drugs that are not included in this "dangerous drug" classification that exhibit all these negative properties.

The confusion has led many critics of our drug laws to argue that the classification is arbitrary and reflects hysterical popular opinion rather than pharmacological and clinical facts. Alcohol, nicotine, and caffeine, as the most telling examples, are not legally classified as drugs, although from a pharmacological and clinical standpoint they most certainly are drugs. At least two of them—alcohol and nicotine—are, in fact, dangerous, more so, it can be demonstrated, than practically all the "dangerous drugs" prohibited by law.

Despite the confusion, however, we can be certain that there is a serious drug problem in the United States. The hard figures on drug use and abuse in America are ominous. It would seem that every man, woman, and child in the country use drugs of one kind or another. Indeed, America leads the world in the per capita ingestion of drugs of all kinds.

Listing these drugs in order of popular preference, we find that alcohol is far and away the leader of the pack, as it has been since the first Europeans set foot on the New World. Although it is not officially classified as such, alcohol has all the attributes of the so-called dangerous drugs save one. It is heavily addicting. The body develops a tolerance for its presence and will not function without this presence once physical addiction is established. Users suffer severe withdrawal symptoms upon abrupt stoppage of alcohol ingestion.

In addition, alcohol is the most intoxicating of drugs. Its depressant action on the critical centers of the brain results in psycho-changes that are more pronounced than that caused by any other drug. This alteration of consciousness, in many cases, triggers antisocial and criminal behavior, causes mental deterioration, and leads to violence to the user or to others.

Finally, alcohol is strongly toxic. It is a protoplasmic poison that attacks the liver, kidneys, heart, and brain. It is a powerful irritant to the mucous membrane, causing damage even with moderate use to the throat, esophagus, and stomach. About the only thing positive that can be said for alcohol is that it makes one feel good when taken in moderation. The one property it does not share with the other "dangerous drugs" is the fact that alcohol is not illegal. One is not sent to jail for possession.

As a social problem, alcohol overshadows all other drugs combined, if only because of the vast number of people involved. Judge Edward J. Dimock, of the U.S. Court for the Southern District of New York, in comparing alcohol addiction with other kinds of drug abuse said: "The tragedy of narcotics, in volume, is but a pale candle flame to the noonday sun compared to the tragedy resulting from the good-natured alcohol with which most of us flirt so gaily. . . ."

In the United States today some 80,000,000 people use alcohol more or less regularly. Out of this number, 65,000,000 are able to regulate their use of the drug satisfactorily. For some 15,000,000, alcohol is a problem, with 6,000,000 to 8,000,000 Americans classified as alcoholics who have lost control of their drinking habit.

These figures are so large that even if alcohol did not have so many negative aspects, it would still overshadow all other forms of drug abuse. Yet the very size of the problem, the sheer volume of people involved take away from the immediacy and drama of the situation. The problem is so large that we no longer notice it. Indeed, alcohol abuse is hardly deviant behavior—it is practically the norm!

The alcohol habit supports a major industry and is an important source of revenue for federal, state, and local governments. Its roots go very deep into the American experience. William Bradford, governor of the Plymouth Colony, complained about the number of drunks staggering about Plymouth at all hours of the day and night some 20 years after the founding of the colony. In the following 300 years, the alcohol problem has kept pace with the population despite temperance movements, religious and social disapproval, and even a constitutional amendment that made alcohol illegal in the United States.

In 1972 the Surgeon General listed about 350,000 deaths in the United States that could be attributed to alcohol. The further cost in broken homes, neglected families, and time lost from work as a result of alcoholism is practically incalculable.

2 I

Despite these drawbacks, however, alcohol remains America's favorite drug, and there seems little likelihood that it will be replaced from this position of dominance in the foreseeable future.

Next in order of preference on this list of America's favorite drug comes tobacco—used regularly by some 55,000,000 people. Tobacco, of course, is not a drug. We all know that. You can buy it in a grocery store! Popular opinion, however, is often deceptive. Although few of us think of it as such, tobacco fills all the pharmacological requirements of a drug, even of an addicting one, though this is denied by some authorities. Tobacco, it is claimed, is not truly addicting—it is merely strongly habit-forming. What this means is that the body does not develop tolerance for nicotine, the active ingredient in tobacco, nor does one suffer withdrawal symptoms upon stopping this use.

Oh, no? Ask any heavy smoker who has either quit or tried to break the habit. He will tell you that tobacco smoking is a powerful addiction with an exquisite array of withdrawal symptoms all its own. It takes all the willpower at one's command to break the habit, and for many it is all but impossible to stop on their own. Even professional help is often resorted to in vain, and people continue smoking despite hypnosis, group therapy, and a thousand other surefire methods to get rid of the habit.

How strong is tobacco addiction?

By now, all of us are aware that smoking is dangerous—it says so on every pack of cigarettes and on every cigarette advertisement:

WARNING: THE SURGEON GENERAL HAS
DETERMINED THAT CIGARETTE SMOKING
IS DANGEROUS TO YOUR HEALTH.

Yet this information has hardly made a dent in the smoking habits of the nation. Indeed, sales figures indicate that the habit is growing despite all warnings. So powerful is this addiction that people go right on smoking while knowing full well that by so doing they are risking death—and a painful, drawn-out, hospital-ridden death at that. According to the Surgeon General's statistics, some 250,000 people in the United States can be expected to die from tobacco-induced maladies this year—80,000 of them as a result of lung cancer!

Cigarette smoking, however, because it is so widespread and common, offers a convenient example of the power of drug addiction. In many respects, it is a prototype for all addiction. Why do people smoke? Even the heaviest smoker would find it difficult to answer this question. Certainly, smoking does not afford any significant physical pleasure. There is no high, no liberating release of inhibition, or even the same kind of physical pleasure provided by a glass of water when one is thirsty. At best, cigarette smoking gives one something to do with his hands at a tense moment, or perhaps, the ritual of the act of lighting up and smoking is psychologically soothing. In any case, it would seem that the physical and psychological benefits are negligible. Yet people continue smoking. They cannot stop despite being aware of the considerable risks involved.

Following close behind tobacco in popularity and perhaps superseding the latter habit—we cannot be certain, however, because precise figures are not available—is the almost universal penchant for "popping" pills. Feeling tired? Take a pill. Can't sleep? Take a pill. Can't stay awake? Take a pill. Nervous and tense? Take a pill. Tired blood? Take a pill. Too fat? Take a pill. Feeling unhappy? Take a pill.

They come in all shapes and sizes: in time-release minicapsules and gaily colored ovals; in tablets and in liquids; in tiny red balls and big green ones. Swallow a pill—it is the only way to deal with those hammers pounding in our heads, lightning bolts shooting into our elbows, and gremlins bowling in our stomachs. And now we are extending this practice of pill popping to include a variety of psychological ills and strains as well.

According to conservative estimates (the AMA in this case), some 40,000,000 to 50,000,000 Americans, possibly more, use sedatives, stimulants, and tranquilizers to help them get through the day. Most of these drugs are obtained legally through doctors' prescriptions and are used for everything from quieting one's nerves to losing weight.

Some, of course, may be bought without prescription, and we are encouraged to do so by multimillion-dollar advertising campaigns. As a result, it is estimated that between 3,000,000 and 5,000,000 people have become addicted to "medicinal" drugs. For them, the daily dose of Nembutal, Miltown, Seconal, or just plain "bennies" has become a necessity that they can no longer do without. They are hooked. They are no more able to face the day without the aid of this crutch than the alcoholic without his gin, the heroin addict without his fix, or the smoker without his cigarette.

Drug manufacturers, with no official restraints to inhibit them, continue to produce these pills with abandon. Last year these companies produced about 100,000 pounds of amphetamines and more than 1,000,000 pounds of barbiturates. This production is estimated to be 35 percent larger than legitimate medical needs would demand. The surplus production often travels a bizarre distribution route, following a circuitous journey into Mexico and Central America, whence the pills return to America and the black market. Too often they end up in our high schools in the grab bag of a teen-age pusher.

As well as manufacturing the product, the drug companies take an additional giant step in creating a demand for their goods. In the best tradition of American business practice, they spend millions on sophisticated advertising campaigns to assure and reinforce this demand by persuading every American that it is medically and socially acceptable to shield himself against all the ordinary hazards of life with chemical aids.

Day after day, in newspapers, on television, in magazines, we are constantly reminded that drugs provide an instant and magical answer to whatever worries or disturbs us. How much difference is there between popping a pill to keep you from "taking it out" on your family or shooting heroin to take the edge off an intolerable ghetto existence? Not very much. This situation of "official drug pushing" was deplored by Dr. Mitchell S. Rosenthal, director of the Phoenix Drug Rehabilitation program in New York City. In his testimony before a Senate hearing, Dr. Rosenthal said:

> While everyone deplores the use of psychoactive drugs by young people, a major industry with practically unlimited access to the mass media has been convincing the American people, young and old alike, that drugs effect instant and significant changes, that, indeed, they work "miracles" such as making a "boring woman" exciting to a husband so that he proclaims her a "new woman"!

Nor have the drug companies neglected the young. In 1972 three major drug companies alone spent some $23,000,000 for television commercials directed specifically to children. Clever advertisements prepared by some of our most prestigious advertising companies urged youngsters to "pop a pill"—vitamin pills in these cases—and "feel better FAST!"

Senator Mike Gravel of Alaska, in testimony before a Senate committee investigating drug abuse, cited the atmosphere of pervasive pill taking as a direct cause of drug abuse. He quoted a recent study that showed that children reared by pill-taking parents are three to ten times more likely to become drug abusers than children whose parents did not take pills regularly.

Addiction to amphetamines and barbiturates has become one of the fastest-growing areas of drug abuse. Many people are introduced to these drugs legitimately through their doctors. Then, because these drugs are comparatively easy to come by, they continue taking the pills without the sanction of their doctor. Both amphetamines and barbiturates are now included in "dangerous drugs" that are proscribed by law, but because both are still freely prescribed by doctors and abundantly produced by manufacturers, it is all but impossible to control the illicit traffic in these drugs. A growing army of abusers continue to take amphetamines to "lift them up" and barbiturates to "bring them down."

Next in order of popularity on our Hit Parade of favorite American drugs comes marijuana—the original "devil's weed!" Although it is classified as a narcotic by government enforcement agencies, the noxious herb has no narcotic qualities whatsoever. It is believed to be a mild stimulant and hallucinogen, though its molecular structure is different from that of all other drugs. Actually, marijuana stands by itself and for all of its sensational reputation hardly qualifies as a drug at all.

All objective, scientific evaluations of marijuana agree that it is not addicting, is only mildly habituating, and clinically has fewer detectable physiological effects than tobacco. Even nutmeg, for that matter, which is mildly hallucinogenic, appears stronger. Marijuana has no deteriorating effects on the brain and none upon the organs of the body.

Indeed, one researcher, Dr. Andrew Weil, who has done considerable work with marijuana, hesitates to classify it as a drug because of the absence of clinical and pharmacological effects. In Dr. Weil's opinion, "the best term for marihuana is active placebo—that is, a substance whose apparent effects on the mind are actually placebo effects in response to minimal physiological action."

Why, if marijuana is clinically and pharmacologically so mild, is it classified as a "dangerous drug"? The answer to this question provides an interesting insight into the process by which our laws are enacted and into the peculiar relationship the American public has with drugs. Actually, the laws regulating marijuana were based upon a hoax, and it can be called nothing less as we shall see in Chapter 5. More peculiar, perhaps, are the reasons why this hoax was accepted so enthusiastically by the American people and their representatives in Congress.

Marijuana also provides an example of the futility of moral legislation. Like the Prohibition laws that made alcohol illegal, the antimarijuana laws have failed in all their avowed purposes. When the first federal antimarijuana law was passed in 1937, the use of this "drug" was limited to a tiny portion of the population. Most people in America had never even heard about the weed.

Since it was made illegal, however, marijuana has flourished mightily. In 1937 an estimated 100,000 to 200,000 people in the United States had ever used marijuana. Today official estimates place the figure at between 25,000,000 and

35,000,000 people who have tried the drug, with some 10,000,000 to 15,000,000 regular users—and the number growing daily! It would seem from this experience that the best way to promote a product is to prohibit it—ban it in Boston, as it were!

Following marijuana on the list of favorite drugs come the psychedelics and hallucinogens, those chemicals that alter the sensual perception and the state of consciousness of the user. Included in this category are LSD, DMT, mescaline, peyote, psilocybin, and psilocin. One of them, peyote, is legal for certain American Indians who use it as a sacrament in their religious rites. Hailed by some researchers as keys to hitherto-inaccessible areas of human consciousness and condemned by others as an illicit source of thrills, the psychedelics include some of the most potent drugs known to man.

LSD, as one example, is so powerful that dosages are measured in micrograms—a microgram is one-millionth of a gram! There are about three grams in an ounce. One ounce of LSD would provide enough of the drug to supply 300,000 individual doses of 200 micrograms. As little as 50 micrograms, however, is enough to trigger a reaction.

Although hallucinogenic drugs are not addicting in the clinical sense—that is, physical tolerance does not develop, and there are no withdrawal symptoms when usage is stopped—they have been included in the list of "dangerous drugs." They are outlawed along with the narcotics, barbiturates, amphetamines, marijuana, and cocaine.

As with marijuana, official prohibition has apparently had little effect. Hallucinogens continue to enjoy a wide popularity, especially among college students, artists, and intellectuals generally, who claim the psychedelic experience is vital in the exploration and experience of different states of consciousness. It has been estimated that at least 3,000,000 Americans have tried LSD, mescaline, or similar psychedelics with some 1,000,000 as more-or-less regular users.

LSD is, of course, a modern drug. It was first synthesized in 1938 by Dr. Albert Hofmann at the Sandoz Laboratories in Switzerland. Its hallucinogenic properties, however, were not discovered until 1943, when Dr. Hofmann accidentally ingested some of the drug and experienced hallucinations. Interest in the drug skyrocketed when Dr. Timothy Leary, then at Harvard University, began experimenting with the drug and extolled its virtues in ecstatic descriptions of LSD-engendered trips.

Although LSD and a number of other synthetic hallucinogens are comparatively new, the natural psychedelics that occur in plants are among the oldest drugs known to man. Laurel leaves, deadly nightshade, henbane, and nutmeg were some of the hallucinogenic plants that were known in Europe, Asia, and Africa from long before recorded history. It was in the New World, however, that this kind of intoxicant reached its highest development.

The Indians of North and South America discovered and developed what was the most extensive pharmacopoeia of hallucinogenic drugs in the world. These drugs, which included mescaline, peyote, psilocybin, jimsonweed, various mushrooms, and other plants, played a central role in the religious life of the American Indians and were used by nearly all the tribes in the New World long before Columbus set sail across the Atlantic in 1492.

At the bottom of our drug list, in order of popularity, if not of notoriety, come the narcotics—those drugs derived from the lovely poppy plant that include opium, morphine, and heroin. Added to these are synthetic opiates such as meperidine, levorphanal, and methadone. These are what law enforcement agencies and the public think of as "hard drugs." The user of these substances is the "dope fiend" of popular mythology, who has sunk so low as to be considered hardly human.

No other form of deviant indulgence receives so much attention or is dealt with so severely by the law. Not as numerous as the drinker or smoker, isolated from the mainstreams of society by a public that looks on him as the complete pariah, the narcotic addict is shunned and despised by all.

In this attitude we find one of the strangest aspects of drug addiction. How do we adequately explain why narcotics addiction is looked upon not merely as a self-limiting or incapacitating habit, such as excessive drinking or smoking, but as a heinous, dehumanizing depravity? Certainly, this marked repugnance cannot stem from the effects of the drug on the user alone. Actually, most laymen are shocked to learn there is very little effect. The picture of the narcotics addict has become hopelessly confused with the reeling, staggering alcoholic drunk. The true picture is very different.

Forty-three years ago George B. Wallace, in reporting on several medical studies made into the effects of opium and its derivatives morphine and heroin on the human body, wrote:

> In carefully planned and conducted studies made at Philadelphia General Hospital and repeated at Bellevue Hospital in New York City, it was shown that continued taking of opium or any of its derivatives resulted in no measurable organic damage. The addict when not deprived of his opium showed no abnormal behavior which distin-

guished him from the non-addict. Further, the most careful examination of his body functions failed to show any damage which could be attributed to the drug.

These findings have never been refuted.

Part of the general revulsion focused on the narcotic addict can be attributed to the press. We have read too many stories of crazed "dope fiends" to remain indifferent. Still, the publicity alone is not enough to explain this almost-universal detestation. Perhaps there is a disturbing sexual symbolism in the act of injecting a substance into the body—a self-violation —that many of us cannot deal with rationally.

Like everything else about narcotics, the number of people addicted is impossible to determine precisely. Today's estimates run from 250,000 to possibly 500,000 or more, according to the source of your figures. Those who have a stake in federal and state drug programs and enforcement plans tend to go with the higher numbers. Those without such a stake tend to quote the lower figure. Although we cannot be certain of the exact figure, we can safely assume that most are exaggerated toward the greater number.

One observer in New York City recently came up with an estimate of 500,000 narcotic addicts in the city who stole some $3.5 billion worth of property annually to support their habit. Now, without doubting the sincerity of the reporter, we question his numbers. He probably meant well and was concerned about a pressing condition, but his figures cannot be accurate. According to the statistics published by the FBI, property theft in the year 1972, not counting automobile thefts, for the entire United States was slightly above $1.5 billion.

Granted that a certain percentage of crime is never reported and does not show up on the statistics, it is still impossible for drug addicts in New York City to have stolen $3.5 billion in any one year or anything remotely approaching that figure. That would come to approximately $400 stolen from every man, woman, and child in the city!

Actually, if another figure that was bandied about in New York City newspaper headlines in October, 1972, was accurate, the $3.5 billion estimate on theft might have been approached. According to a report made by the Fleischmann Committee which was investigating New York City schools, *45 percent of all students in high schools and junior high schools were on drugs!* We always knew that New York City schools were high—but this is ridiculous!

Despite the exaggerations and alarmist headlines, there is a narcotics problem in the United States—a very serious one. There are about 300,000 addicts in the country (probably less, but possibly more) who must have their daily "fix." Now a society with a population of more than 200,000,000 should be able to absorb the negative effects of even 300,000 addicts without too much trouble. We should, but unfortunately we do not. Pick up any newspaper, read any magazine, and the stories about narcotics, addicts, and enforcement of related laws will confirm this national failure.

The principal problem, however, does not stem from the effects of the drugs themselves on the user as from the fact that they are illegal. Outside of being highly addictive, narcotics do negligible physical and psychological damage to the user. The criminalization of narcotics, on the other hand, has had deadly effect.

For one thing, criminalization drives the price of drugs up

dramatically. A daily dose for the typical addict that should cost no more than a few cents a day goes up to $50 a day and more. Not very many people can afford to sustain such a regular expense, and so most addicts are compelled to steal, become prostitutes or drug pushers themselves in order to support their habit. The end result is crime waves in all our major cities perpetrated by addicts who must raise the money to supply themselves with drugs.

More serious than the crime engendered by narcotics addiction is the fact that there is no quality control on illegally obtained drugs. The buyer has no way of knowing what he is buying and no redress for fraud or the purchase of adulterated goods. He cannot, after all, call the Better Business Bureau. In most cases the drug content of the "bags" sold on the street is so low that the addict tends to overestimate the extent of his addiction. Should he obtain a bag with a comparatively pure content there is always the chance of death by overdose.

To round out this survey of the contemporary drug scene we have such esoterica as glue sniffing, cocaine and inhalation of amyl nitrite and nitrous oxide. The general method of ingesting glue is sticking one's head into a paper bag in which airplane glue has been spread over the bottom. Amyl nitrite is a clear, yellow, volatile liquid that comes in glass ampuls that are broken open into a handkerchief and inhaled. A relaxant, it is used medically to relieve the pain of angina pectoris. Nitrous oxide is, of course, the familiar "laughing gas" used as an anesthetic for minor surgery and dental work.

Finally, there is cocaine, a powerful natural stimulant whose use is apparently growing rapidly. In its pure form, cocaine is a white crystalline powder that is generally sniffed or injected for its almost violent stimulating effects. The source

33

of this drug is an alkaloid contained in the leaves of the coca bush, which is grown in Bolivia, Peru, Chile, and Java. Most of the cocaine in illicit traffic originates in these countries.

This completes the picture of our drug scene today. At best it is confusing and contradictory. It would seem that our view of drugs in America is rather peculiar and resembles what we might see in Alice's "Looking Glass." We have what Dr. Helen Nowlis, author of *Drugs on the College Campus*, describes as a "magic potion" concept of drugs. If they are "good," they can do no harm. "Bad" drugs, on the other hand, can do no good. "Bad," of course, is defined as nonmedically indicated and taken merely for (gasp!) *pleasure.*

If one were to look for purely pharmacological reasons for labeling one drug "dangerous" and another "safe," he would be hard pressed to find any medical reason. One researcher in this field, Dr. Samuel Irwin, has compiled a list of drugs that are commonly used in order of their physical danger to the taker. When we compare this list to that compiled in the "dangerous drug" laws, we find a huge medical discrepancy: (1) glue sniffing; (2) methamphetamine; (3) alcohol; (4) cigarettes; (5) barbiturates; (6) heroin and related narcotics; (7) LSD and other hallucinogens; (8) marijuana.

The arbitrary nature of legal classification of drugs into legal and illegal categories has led Dr. Thomas Szasz, professor of psychiatry at Syracuse Medical Center, to say outrightly: "Since most of the propaganda against drug abuse seeks to justify certain repressive policies by appeals to the alleged danger of certain drugs, the propagandists often must falsify the facts about the true pharmacological properties of the drugs they seek to prohibit. . . ."

This situation begs the question: How did it get that way? To answer that interesting query, we must look back upon the long history of drugs in America and to the strange views the American public has always held toward drugs. Contrary to what most of us may think, drugs are not a new problem in this country. Drug taking goes back to the tobacco patches of the Indians and their use of such psychedelics as peyote, mushrooms, and jimsonweed to bring about a state of religious trance.

The Pilgrims brought ample supplies of "spirits" to the New World and made rum an integral part of their commercial life. Along with "spirits" came vials of laudanum—tincture of opium—that straitlaced Puritan ladies sipped to relieve the pain of rheumatism, stomach upset . . . and just living. In the 1850's America could even boast of a Hashish Club where writers and artists gathered to turn on and attempt to outdo the visions of their stylish counterparts in Paris.

The Civil War brought in its wake a wave of morphine addiction, or "soldier's disease," as it was commonly called. Morphine was used as an analgesic in hypodermic injection for the first time in the treatment of soldiers wounded in battle. At the turn of the century a Harvard psychologist named William James was turning on with nitrous oxide and extolling its religious significance long before another Harvard psychologist named Tomothy Leary began tripping with LSD.

Nor is this predilection for drugs in any way a peculiarly American failing. Drugs are as old as man, and there are even examples of drug use among animals. Indeed, it could be argued that the compulsion to change or alter a state of consciousness is a biological need, inbuilt into the life forms that have evolved upon this planet Earth.

What appears to be unique about the drug scene in America today is the fact that it is changing so quickly. Within the past decade there appears to have been a revolution in preferred intoxicants. Drugs that were used by only a tiny fraction of the population before this time are now tried by millions of Americans—most of them young. It is this cultural mutation that has caught the nation by surprise. Perhaps if we go back and review the long history of drugs in America, we may be able to approach the problem more rationally—if not less emotionally.

2.

BEFORE COLUMBUS

DRUGS did not first come to the Western Hemisphere with European explorers and settlers. They were here, in abundance, long before white men arrived. Without the help of Europeans, the American Indians had developed what was probably the most elaborate and sophisticated array of psychedelic and hallucinogenic drugs known to man. There was, however, no "drug problem" in the sense that we understand it today. This aspect of the drug culture came with the Europeans. Some of the most potent drugs known to man were made part of Indian life with little or no disruption of the social fabric. The hallucinogenic experience was central to the religious life of all the people who lived in what is now North and South America.

When Columbus first came into sight of the New World, North America was sparsely inhabited by a race of men who had struck an enviable balance with their environment. There were, at most, 2,000,000 to 3,000,000 people scattered throughout the vast area that now encompasses the United States and Canada. They were divided into independent tribes, each with its own customs, language, and traditions. These were the people of the forests and the plains. They were hunters and food gatherers who were just beginning to make agriculture economically important to their existence.

In Mexico and South America the population was considerably larger, and high levels of civilization were achieved in both these areas. The Aztec and Mayan cultures of Mexico and the Incan of South America were similar in many respects of organization, architectural achievements, and intellectual, artistic, and religious development to the Egyptian and Sumerian civilizations of Africa and the Near East. Indeed, the Inca civilization of South America supported a larger population at a higher standard of living than anything achieved in some 300 years of Spanish colonial rule. It is only now, in the latter part of the twentieth century, that the Inca levels are beginning to be approached once more.

We are, however, more concerned with that portion of continental North America that is north of the Rio Grande. Here the tribes were small and had not achieved the organizational levels of the Mexican and South American populations. The Mohawk, for example, who lived in what is now central New York State and who played such a significant role in the history of the colonial period, numbered no more than about 10,000 individuals at the height of the tribe's population and influence.

This tribe, the Mohawk, was, in fact, the largest in the northeast. Most tribes were much smaller. More typical were the Mohican, who lived in parts of what is now Westchester County in New York and nearby Connecticut, or the Canarsie Indians who lived in what is now part of Brooklyn. Neither tribe ever numbered more than 1,500 individuals.

The Indians encountered by the early French and English

settlers of North America were of mixed Algonquian and Iroquoian stock (these names refer to linguistic groups rather than confederations). Within each division there were numerous tribes that had no political connection with each other. Only the five Iroquois Nations—Cayuga, Mohawk, Oneida, Onondaga, and Seneca—had joined together into anything resembling a federation.

These tribes lived, for the most part, by hunting; fishing and shellfish digging; cultivation of corn, squash, and beans; and the gathering of wild nuts, fruits, and berries. Their level of economic and cultural development was roughly equivalent to that of the Neolithic period—a stage the ancestors of the European settlers had gone through some 4,000 or 5,000 years earlier.

Most of the eastern tribes were semisedentary. That is, they erected villages and cultivated farms, but these were, at best, semipermanent arrangements. As game grew scarce in one area or the land became unproductive, the Indians merely packed their few possessions and moved to a more promising site. In the vast, empty reaches of North America there was more than enough room for all. There were no permanent villages, cities, or towns in the European sense.

There were, however, definite centers for trading and meeting that were well defined and recognized as such by most tribes in the area. Manhattan Island, as one example, was a place where different tribes from the surrounding areas came to exchange goods, socialize, and meet on neutral ground, as it were, to resolve any tribal disputes and arguments. One of its Indian names was *Laaphamachkineg,* which, roughly translated, means place of wampum trading—wampum, of course, was a principal medium of exchange among eastern Indian tribes, equivalent in many respects to our money.

Tribal settlements were often enclosed by a wooden palisade as protection against raids by neighboring tribes. Intertribal warfare—often of an almost ritualistic nature—was a characteristic feature of Indian life. Within the palisades the Indians lived in longhouses, each of which sheltered a maternally lineated clan that sometimes included as many as fifteen individual families. Each longhouse was decorated on the gabled ends with a painted crest that represented the family clan.

The longhouse was the basic unit of Indian society. These extended households of blood lineage were projected into clans, the clans into moieties, moieties into tribes or nations. Kinship and family loyalty was the basis of political life. Every community had its council of adult males chosen by the people of the village, who counseled the village chiefs. There were chiefs for various aspects of tribal life. The peace chief, for example, was concerned with civil affairs of the village and was elected by the women. The war chief, on the other hand, was chosen by the men to lead them in battle.

Speakers of the council were called pine tree chiefs and had earned the right to voice their opinions at council meetings through merit exhibited in hunting, warfare, or trading expeditions with other tribes or villages. In the protocol of these primitive societies, the speakers elected the hunting and war chiefs.

Council meetings seem to have been a favored pastime of the Indians. They spent an inordinate amount of time at such meetings, which were held for every occasion from spring planting to fall hunting. One such meeting held by a Mohawk village was described by J. F. Lafitau, a French Jesuit who lived among them for a number of years during the latter part of the seventeenth century:

... a greasy assemblage, the braves sitting on their haunches, crouched like apes, their knees as high as their ears, or lying, some on their backs, some on their stomachs, each with a pipe in his mouth, discussing affairs of state with as much coolness and gravity as the Spanish Junta or the Grand Council of Venice. ...

This reference to the participants of a council meeting each with "a pipe in his mouth" by a Jesuit priest is significant. The smoking of a pipe was traditional at all Indian meetings and councils. The Indians believed that no important decision should be made without first cooling tempers and clearing the mind with a contemplative smoke of an appropriate herb. On some occasions the Indians smoked tobacco. On others they put dried jimson leaves in their calumet bowls, or sumac leaves, or laurel or henbane, or any one of a variety of hallucinogenic plants they had discovered.

Tobacco was smoked in the famed peace pipe that marked the end of hostilities between tribes. Other leaves were smoked during a period of contemplation and meditation that preceded all important tribal decisions and meetings. Still others were smoked in association with religious ceremonies and rituals. These hallucinogenic experiences were woven into the fabric of Indian social life to an extent that would be difficult for us to imagine today.

A typical forest village consisted of anywhere from 50 to 200 people who lived in some five to ten longhouses. Such groups were the primary economic and social units of the forest culture. Tribes were loose associations of such villages that were related by matrilineal bloodlines, a common language, and customs.

Occupations in the villages were divided between the sexes.

Gangs of men built houses, erected palisades, fished, hunted, traveled, traded, participated in intertribal games, defended the villages, made war on neighboring tribes, made music, did all the carving and decorating of the longhouses. Women did the farming, made clothing, wove baskets and containers, looked after the children, gathered wild foodstuffs, dug clams and oysters, and generally controlled the civil affairs of the villages.

Although never extensive in most of North America, agriculture played a basic role in the economy of the tribe. In fields that were either burned over to remove timber or in natural meadows, generally situated close to the villages, parties of women, each directed by a matron, worked the fields. They grew corn, squash, beans, and other vegetables, plus tobacco, morning glory, jimson, and other plants that were cultivated for their psychedelic properties. These plots of land worked by the women of the village generally averaged about three or four acres per longhouse.

After the fall harvest, in which the men participated, hunting parties left the villages and ranged far into the forests in search of game for meat and furs. The men generally did not return to the villages until midwinter, when the entire village joined together for one of the most important festivals of the Indian year.

For several weeks in early spring, entire villages moved to the migration routes of the now-extinct passenger pigeons. These birds, which numbered in the billions, gathered into migrating flocks, which stretched for miles in dense clouds that darkened the sky. Indians took prodigious quantities of these pigeons, which provided a staple of their diet. Spring runs of fish also drew villagers to nearby streams, rivers, and lake inlets to erect traps and weirs for the capture of fish. Old women and children gathered spring greens and roots to tide them over the hungry period before the first berries ripened.

In retrospect, the life of these people seems almost idyllic to us today. There was no crime, no poverty, and no alienation in the sense that we know these things today. Everyone belonged; everyone had a respected place and purpose within the life of the tribe. Like the wolf or deer of the forest, the Indians were in harmony with nature. They lived gently on the land and left few scars to mark their existence.

Like all primitive peoples, however, their lives were severely circumscribed by religion, ceremony, and superstition. They lived in a magical world where every occurrence was supernatural. Life was a constant struggle to control and influence baleful emanations of the spirits. This control was exercised through ceremony and ritual. There was a ceremony for every occasion, from the start of a hunting expedition to the birth of a child, from preparations for war to the planting of the corn. Ceremony and religion were entwined into every aspect of tribal life.

Although the tribes of North America differed greatly in language, customs, and manner of living, religious life was much the same over vast areas of the continent. There were, of course, regional differences and local gods and totems, but the overall religious outlook was similar throughout this vast area. The American Indians lived in a world that was pervaded by spirit to an extent that would be difficult for us to appreciate today. Spirit was everywhere. It resided in trees, flowers, animals, rocks, streams, rivers, birds, and even insects.

In one respect, at least, Indian religion revealed a higher moral sense than the European. In the Indian view, all nature was imbued with sanctity, and with sanctity comes respect. When an Indian slew a deer or chopped down a tree, he did so only after ceremonially propitiating its spirit, and even then he probably felt a twinge of remorse at the act.

The Christian, of course, has no such compunctions. In the Judeo-Christian tradition nature is given to man to be dominated and exploited:

> Be fruitful, and multiply, and replenish the earth, and subdue it; and have dominion over the fish of the seas, and over the fowl of the air, and over every living thing that moveth upon the earth. . . . Behold, I have given you every herb yielding seed, which is upon the face of all the earth, and every tree. . . .

The effects of this moral blindness are now being felt throughout the world in the critical despoliation of the environment which threatens the very existence of man.

Central to the religious experience of the American Indian was the vision: the ecstatic, hallucinatory moment when all mystery is revealed; the trance wherein the everyday world is transcended for a brief moment of mystic glory. Because it was so important in their religious life, all Indians placed a high value on trances, ecstatic hallucinations, and transcending vertigo. In their view, such states were divine. They connoted a quasi-magical power over the environment, a supernal self-aggrandizement, a glorious intimacy with the universe.

To arrive at this exalted state was the worthiest of goals, and the Indians developed a variety of techniques to achieve this end. Some resorted to fasting and self-torture—practices already familiar as religious exercises leading to mystic experience. Others relied on mass dancing, singing, and chanting—techniques also familiar to the European religious experience. Still others reached this desired state through the use of drugs—peyote, mescaline, morning glory seeds, tobacco, mushrooms, henbane, coca leaf, laurel, sumac, atropine derived from plants of the potato family, mandrake, thorn apple, and a host of other hallucinogenic plants and herbs all known to induce that glorious ecstasy, that "holy reeling of the mind," so highly valued by the Indians.

William James, the Harvard psychologist who turned on with drugs some seventy years before Timothy Leary of LSD notoriety, was greatly impressed with this Indian preoccupation with religious intoxication. In his book *The Varieties of Religious Experience*, James cited the Papago Indians of Arizona who "hymn the glories of dizziness." He then goes on to say that the words in the Papago language which mean drunken and dizzy are "sacred and poetic, for the trance of drunkenness is akin to the trance of vision in their experience."

With such a religious bias, it is not surprising that the American Indians developed a variety of trance-inducing drugs. These psychedelic substances were used regularly by all members of the various tribes in religious ceremonies and in all important rites of passage. Drug-induced trances were part of birth and death rites; they were used in ceremonies that marked the introduction of youths to adulthood, in marriages, and at all the festivals that marked the Indian year. Sacred drugs were used by all—men, women, and children—and were considered an indispensable part of religious life.

There were also adepts in Indian society—shamans, witch doctors, or medicine men—who were the equivalent of European priests and holy men. For them, drugs played a different role from that of most other people. A remarkable series of books written by Carlos Castaneda, an anthropologist who describes his experiences with an Indian shaman, offers

45

an invaluable insight into this special world of the Indian adept.

Carlos Castaneda apprenticed himself to Don Juan, a Yaqui Indian shaman (brujo) from northern Mexico, who initiated him into the mysteries associated with a number of the psychedelic plants of the southwest. Don Juan introduced Castaneda to an ancient tradition that had obviously been passed down from generation to generation of southwestern Indians.

For the brujo (or man of knowledge, as Don Juan described himself) drugs played a unique role. They were methods, techniques for entering and exploring an area of human consciousness that is generally unavailable to normal experience. Psychedelic drugs, according to the teachings of Don Juan, provide a key, an entrance into this "separate reality" which is identical to the mystic state recognized by all religions.

In time, however, the man of knowledge, Don Juan makes it clear, can dispense with drugs and enter the exalted, mystic state through the exercise of will alone. Drugs, then, are merely part of a discipline that allows the adept entrance into this particular area of consciousness. This entrance, in turn, creates the man of knowledge, who has an entire area of reality available to him that ordinary men cannot be aware of through their limited consciousness.

Among the drugs that were first used by American Indians is one that has spread to all corners of the world since its introduction. This drug, of course, is tobacco. Europeans were first introduced to this aromatic plant and the technique of ingesting the drug through the inhalation of smoke from the smoldering leaves when Columbus brought some back to the court of Spain.

The subsequent spread of tobacco smoking throughout the world is one of the most remarkable phenomena in the history of drugs. It was almost as though the rest of the world were waiting for the introduction of this marvelous leaf and this novel method of ingesting it. For smoking—the actual breathing in of fumes from a burning substance—was an American invention.

There had been from antiquity examples of breathing smoke from a smoldering fire to ingest drugs. The burning of incense is one such example. Another, of course, was the Delphic oracle in ancient Greece, where a priestess breathed in the smoke of laurel leaves burning on an altar and fell into a prophetic trance. The actual act of smoking, however, the technique of bringing the substance for ingestion to the lips and inhaling the smoke directly, was unknown in the rest of the world before its introduction by American Indians.

From a pharmacological viewpoint, smoking is the most efficient method for ingesting a drug outside of direct injection into the bloodstream. In the lungs, where blood is oxygenated before continuing its circulation through the body, the substance inhaled also enters directly into the bloodstream.

Some of the more potent Indian drugs are coming into vogue. Peyote, of course, is still used legally by American Indians throughout the Southwest in religious rites. This is also the drug that was lauded by Aldous Huxley in his book *Doors to Perception*, which has had so great an influence on the contemporary drug scene.

Cocaine is another potent drug that has come to us from the Americas. This preparation originated in South America and is the alkyd of the coca plant, which is still chewed by millions of South American Indians in Bolivia, Peru, Chile, and

Argentina. It acts as a mild stimulant, and the Indians claim that it counteracts the effects of fatigue and hunger.

Sigmund Freud, of psychoanalytic fame, also used cocaine. He was so impressed with the mind-expanding qualities of the drug that for a time he argued that it might be an indispensable tool in the treatment of neurosis.

The one drug that never came into wide use in the Western Hemisphere before the advent of Europeans was alcohol. It was not entirely unknown in the New World before Columbus, but its use was limited. In Mexico some of the tribes had developed beers brewed from corn, and other Indians had learned to ferment maguey sap into an alcoholic beverage of about 50 proof. Throughout most of North America, however, neither squash, rich in carbohydrates, and corn nor the abundant wild grapes and berries had been exploited for their alcoholic potential.

When Europeans introduced distilled spirits to the North American Indians, the effects were cataclysmic. These primitive people in whose religion trance and intoxication played so important a role, succumbed helplessly to this European drug which is the most intoxicating substance known to man. As with smallpox and tuberculosis, the Indians had no natural resistance to European drugs. They could not resist the heady lure of alcohol.

Spirits, largely in the form of crude, ill-tasting whiskey, became the principal item in trade with the Indians. Spirits were what the Indians wanted. They would rather have a keg of whiskey than textiles, hardware, or even firearms and gunpowder. European traders and merchants, in this case, were not reluctant to give the Indians what they wanted.

Besides, whiskey in compact kegs that were easily carried over rough trails and portages was more inexpensively delivered to the Indians than other trade goods. These kegs of whiskey found their way to the most remote Indian villages. There they were emptied as soon as physically possible. The Indian aim in drinking was apparently to get himself reeling, blind, passing-out drunk as soon as possible.

European doctors marveled at the Indian passion for whiskey. One doctor described it as the congenital drug addiction of a whole race. Yet this passion was not limited to the red man. In the Pacific islands the Polynesians, who also had not known alcohol, behaved in a similar fashion when they first encountered spirits. Donald Horton, an anthropologist who has studied this problem among primitive peoples, said: "Moderate drinking in the European sense is relatively rare . . . drinking to excess is characteristic of primitive people."

Here was a people who were able to manage some of the most varied and sophisticated psychedelic drugs known, completely helpless in the face of alcohol. This gift of Europe was one of the most destructive forces in the subsequent dissolution of Indian tribal life.

Actually, this meeting of a primitive with a comparatively advanced people proved disastrous. The mystic dreamers of the forests were no match for the alcohol-swilling, Bible-thumping, aggressively murderous Europeans. Within 150 years of the advent of Europeans to North America, the ruin of the seaboard tribes was almost total, and that of the trans-Appalachian tribes ominously advanced. European diseases and superior arms took a frightful toll of the forest people, and alcohol debauched the rest. Eyewitness accounts from the period offer a poignant picture of this race of men literally drinking itself to death.

The Seneca, as one example, once a proud member of the

Five Nation Iroquois Confederacy, expired in drunken, murderous debacle. They lived in what is now the border region between New York and Pennsylvania in the Allegheny Mountains. Each year they carried their annual catch of beaver, muskrat, and other furs down the Allegheny River to Pittsburgh. There they traded their catch for whiskey, which they brought back to their villages. For days and weeks thereafter, until every keg was drunk empty, their home villages became scenes of murderous alcoholic frenzy and intratribal riot between both sexes. A horrified witness at one such debauch described a whole village gone mad. Husbands attacked wives, bashing in their heads with clubs. Mothers threw children into the fires or drowned them in the rivers. No people could survive such orgies for long.

Benjamin Franklin, who witnessed a similar scene after an intertribal council near what is now Carlisle, Pennsylvania, described the debacle in his *Autobiography*: "Their dark-colored bodies half naked, seen only by the gloomy light of the bonfires, running after and beating one another with firebrands, formed a scene that most resembled hell that could well be imagined. . . ."

The Indians, of course, tried to fight back. Leader after leader arose who exhorted the people to resist the temptation of the white man's rum. Their efforts, alas, were too little and too late. The Indian's own religious practices had sealed his doom and made it all but impossible for the red man to resist alcohol. Ecstasy, trance, vertigo—these states of consciousness were held in the highest esteem by the forest people.

When these states were obtained through ingestion of the comparatively mild psychedelics, Indian society was able to regulate and control their use. Hallucinogenic drugs were part of practically every aspect of Indian life. The Indians, however, proved helpless in the face of the more potent alcohol.

The Indian yearned for ecstasy and transcendence and did not care whence it came. Alcohol promised all. One good swig to start with and no reluctance to lose self-control, no fear of disaster to his own interests or those of his family, and the Indian was on the way. There were no solitary drinkers among the red men; once opened, a keg of whiskey was shared by all until empty, without remorse or shame. For in the pragmatic view of the Indian what shame could there be in being whirled out of oneself so gloriously?

This picture of a proud and dignified people destroying itself through drink has left an indelible picture on the American experience. The drunkenness of the Indians surviving on Long Island in the early nineteenth century was one of the things that set Lyman Beecher against the evils of alcohol. Later the same hapless people moved Walt Whitman to write of the "awful lesson which may be learned from the consequences of the burning firewater upon the Indians."

It also left an example of the destructive power of drugs once men lose control over their use.

3. DEMON RUM

As PART of its educational program, the PTA chapter of a Brooklyn high school recently held a meeting in which the drug problem would be the topic of discussion. This was not an unusual event. Similar meetings have been organized in practically every high school in America as part of a nationwide effort to alert parents to a danger that appears to be spreading among schoolchildren all over the country. The principal speaker at this meeting was a drug counselor associated with the school.

In his talk, the counselor emphasized the sad fact that schoolchildren today are confronted with temptations of a far more sinister nature than ever before. Dramatically, he told the assembled parents that before their children were graduated from high school, all of them, without exception, would have been offered marijuana, amphetamines, barbiturates, LSD, and even heroin. "This," he said, "is a fact of life in the United States in the year 1973." The audience gasped at the thought of the modern perils besetting their children.

Then the speaker contrasted these contemporary entice-ments with those of his youth and, presumably, that of his audience. "All we had to worry about when we were kids," he said humorously, "was beer on Saturday night—and maybe a little whiskey for those of us who were really daring." The parents responded by laughing at this allusion to the compara-tive innocence of *their* youths.

Alas, both the statement of the speaker and the laughter of the audience were inappropriate. Old "Demon Rum" is no laughing matter. Although the perils of alcohol appear to have been overshadowed by temptations on a new order, that appearance is deceptive. Alcohol, in fact, remains far and away the most dangerous, the most damaging, and the most costly addictive drug in America and the world today by any standard of measurement. We take it for granted, and most of us do not even think of alcohol as an addictive drug; but the facts reveal a different picture.

The number of alcohol addicts (alcoholics) in America today is staggering. According to a formula developed by E. M. Jellinek, who has studied the problem for decades, between 3 and 4 percent of the population of America can be classified as alcoholic. Thus, between 6,000,000 and 8,000,000 people are afflicted, with some 4,000,000 or 5,000,000 more for whom drinking is a serious problem. Americans spend some $12 billion annually for alcoholic beverages, making this one of the most important industries in the country.

The cost in lives lost as a result of alcoholism, as one more statistical index to the scope of the problem, is more than triple the deaths attributed to all other drugs combined, tobacco excepted. Some 350,000 deaths a year are caused by alcohol—either as a result of the physiological damage that prolonged ingestion inflicts upon the organs of the body or through accidents caused by drunkenness and alcoholic neglect.

Had the speaker been better informed, perhaps, he might have mentioned the fact that the chances of becoming addicted to alcohol are some forty times greater than the chances of becoming addicted to any other drug. From a psychological and physiological viewpoint, all addictions are basically the same. The heroin addict and the alcoholic both are tied to their respective drug by powerful bonds. Both appear helpless in the face of an insatiable need.

All this is by way of saying that our attitudes toward drugs are anything but rational. Too often these attitudes are based on myths, half-truths, sensational stories dreamed up by writers, and a puritanical heritage that still looks on pleasure as suspect. Rarely are these attitudes based on fact—if only because the facts in this area are so difficult to come by. Worse yet, most of the laws that govern the use of drugs appear to be based on the same criteria as our attitudes.

Alcohol, for example, though it is probably the most dangerous addictive of all from a physiological standpoint, is our national intoxicant and as such does not illicit the hysteria we display toward other, less familiar drugs. We have lived too long and intimately with this old demon to permit the same kind of scare reaction so many of us experience when we consider heroin, LSD, or marijuana. Although most of us are aware of the dangers inherent in alcohol, we do not panic when we hear the word spoken.

"Sure, alcohol kills, and a lot of people cannot handle it; but we can say the same thing about cars. In both cases we should do everything possible to alert people to the dangers and minimize them as best we can." This, effectively, is the attitude most Americans take toward alcohol today, by and large a sensible one.

Not too long ago, however, this attitude was different. At one time alcohol illicited the same fear and hysteria we feel toward heroin today. Indeed, alcohol was outlawed in the United States. For a time the manufacture, sale, and transportation of alcoholic beverages were crimes, punishable by law. The Volstead Act, the enforcing arm of the Eighteenth Amendment was passed by Congress on October 28, 1919, over a veto by President Woodrow Wilson. It made any beverage with an alcoholic content of more than $\frac{1}{2}$ of 1 percent illegal. The law remained in effect for almost fourteen years until it was repealed on December 5, 1933, when Congress ratified the Twenty-first Amendment.

The Volstead Act failed because people in America did not stop drinking under Prohibition. Drinking merely became a crime—by virtue of an act of Congress. As a result, a whole new criminal class arose in the United States, a class that numbered in the tens of millions. Certainly, this posed an unwieldy legal situation. It became very difficult to prosecute, no less jail the estimated one-third of the population that openly flouted the law. The law, of course, failed. What this experience demonstrated was the fact that our national drug was not something to be trifled with, even by the most well-meaning people. Alcohol proved to be too firmly entrenched in the collective psyche of America to be eradicated by legislation and the threat of legal punishment. Its roots went too deep.

Alcohol is the great contribution of Europe to the drug spectrum of the world. Although this is one of our most ancient drugs, known from antiquity, whose use was almost universal —the exceptions being North America and some of the

Polynesian islands, where alcohol was apparently unknown until its introduction by Europeans—it was in Europe that it enjoyed its widest popularity and most complete development. In the Moslem world, for example, the use of alcohol was effectively restricted by prohibitions in the Koran. Similar religious restraints discouraged its use in India and China.

Alcohol itself is a complex hydrocarbon whose potable form (ethyl alcohol) has the chemical formula C_2H_5OH. It occurs as a by-product of the natural fermentation of grains and fruits that are rich in carbohydrates. Chemically, it can be considered a derivative of water (HOH) in which one hydrogen atom is replaced by the ethyl molecule (C_2H_5). Unfortunately —or fortunately, as the case may be—this hydrocarbon reacts with the body in a startling manner. Readily entering the bloodstream through the walls of the stomach and intestines, it quickly rises to high levels. Minutes after drinking two ounces of 90 proof whiskey, the blood level of alcohol in a 165-pound man will measure some .05 percent.

Once it enters the bloodstream, alcohol is distributed throughout the body, where it reacts toxically with most of the internal organs. It is when alcohol reaches the brain, however, that the most interesting processes begin. There its toxic properties act as a depressant. In a complicated interaction, the presence of alcohol in the brain tends to inhibit the normal functions. This inhibition is selective in the sense that different areas of the brain are progressively affected. The first area affected is the cerebral cortex which controls the so-called higher functions rather than the semiautomatic ones. Thus, a driver under the influence of a moderate dose of alcohol may be able to drive at his usual speed, but he will tend to make more mistakes.

The more complex functions of the brain, those involved

with judgment, self-criticism, the inhibitions instilled from childhood, are depressed first. The loss of these mental controls results, in most people, in a feeling of elation and euphoria in the early stages of intoxication. One physician described this stage like this: "Alcohol does not make people do things better; it makes them less ashamed of doing them badly."

With the ingestion of more alcohol, the inhibition of function spreads to progressively larger areas of the brain. If enough alcohol is consumed, the entire brain will become anesthetized, and death will ensue from failure of the autonomous functions which control respiration, digestion, and temperature control. Fortunately, though such deaths occur, they are rare. The drinker generally passes out before he can ingest enough alcohol to reach this stage of complete paralysis. Loss of consciousness automatically stops his drinking.

Physiologically, alcohol is the most damaging and dangerous of all addictive drugs. It acts as an irritant to the mucous membrane that lines the throat and esophagus, thus creating the hoarseness of voice so characteristic of the alcoholic. In the stomach, it attacks the lining, leaving the heavy drinker prone to ulcers and other stomach ailments. It attacks the liver and kidneys, constricts the blood vessels, and impairs the action of the heart. In short, alcohol acts as a poison affecting all the vital systems of the body.

The initial feeling of elation and euphoria which accompanies the early stages of intoxication in most people, however, is what makes alcohol so attractive. It is the most intoxicating drug available to man. Its depressant effect on the higher functions of the brain result in what many experience as a liberating release from constricting inhibitions and conscience.

It is this release, presumably, that struck so responsive a chord in the psyches of Europeans. From Russia to Spain and from Italy to Scotland, Europeans developed a variety of alcoholic beverages. With the perfection of efficient distilling techniques in the twelfth century, which permitted a concentration of alcohol of 50 percent and more (as contrasted with the 14 percent concentrate in wines and ciders and the 4 percent concentrate in beers and ales), Europe embarked on an alcoholic binge that continues to this day.

In the beginning, it must be remembered, distilled spirits were looked on as nothing short of miraculous. The alchemists who first distilled it in potable quantities called alcohol *aqua vitae*—water of life—and attributed wondrous properties to this potent fluid. At first, it was thought of and used primarily as a medicine—one of the world's first "wonder drugs."

One English physician of the fourteenth century was so enthusiastic about the properties of alcohol that he hailed it as a panacea for practically all of man's earthly ills:

> It sloweth age; it strengtheneth youth; it helpeth digestion; it cutteth flegme; it abandoneth melancholie; it relisheth the hearte; it lighteneth the minde; it keepeth and preserveth the head from whirling, the eyes from dazzling, the tonge from lisping, the mouth from snaffling, the teeth from chattering, and the throat from rattling.

When quaffed, it seemed to warm the mouth and throat with a painless fire, and once swallowed, it diffused through the body and soul a feeling of heightened well-being that was too easily mistaken for an intensification of life itself. The euphoria that accompanied the drinking of spirits was associated, at first, with the divine and was looked on as a blessing from God Himself, denied the infidel unbelievers. In time, all Europe, or so it seemed, was afloat on a sea of alcohol.

This European taste was not left behind when Spaniards, Portuguese, and later Frenchmen, Englishmen, and Dutchmen settled in the New World. Wine and brandy were staples on Spanish, Portuguese, and French ships, and Dutchmen never ventured far without their daily ration of *genever* (gin). In the diary kept aboard the *Arabella*, which carried Puritan passengers to the Massachusetts Bay Colony, one entry mentions a servant girl who "near killed herself" by taking too liberal a dose of "strong waters" against the seasickness.

Nor were Old World prejudices abandoned in the New. One of the strongest was a marked distrust for water as a beverage. This distrust was based, in part, on sound hygienic principle. The water supplies in most European cities of the time were not particularly reliable, and the risk of pollution was high. In many places it was downright dangerous to drink the water. Another reason for this distrust may have been the mistaken notion, based upon homeopathic analogy, that confused the strength of one's body with the strength of one's drink. Water—thin, flavorless, without color—was suspected of diluting bodily strength, whereas it stood to reason that "spirits" warmed and strengthened.

Finally, an economic snobbishness heightened this New World hydrophobia. To have only plain water to drink was a confession of poverty. When reduced to this extreme, the self-respecting colonist invariably mixed molasses, sugar, or even vinegar into his water to mask the implied disgrace. Water was suitable only for cooking. It was not meant for drinking. A song written by Benjamin Franklin (*circa* 1745) typifies the colonial attitude:

> . . . 'Twas honest old Noah first planted the Vine,
> And mended his Morals by drinking its Wine;

And justly the drinking of water decry'd;
For he knew that all Mankind, by drinking it dy'd. . . .

From this piece of History plainly we find
That Water's good neither for Body nor Mind;
That Virtue & Safety in Wine-bibbing's found
While all that drink Water deserve to be drown'd. . . .

With these attitudes prevalent in the New World, it is not surprising that American colonists took to alcohol with what we would now consider excessive enthusiasm. Indeed, the per capita consumption of alcoholic beverages in colonial America was staggering (literally) by our standards today. Although completely reliable figures from the time are not available, one estimate that comes down to us from the period is revealing. In tallying up his figures, the owner of a tavern in Stockbridge, Massachusetts, calculated that in one year he sold the equivalent of eleven quarts of rum for every man, woman, and child in the town. This, of course, was only the amount bought and drunk in the tavern. It did not include the drinking done at home.

In another Massachusetts town, a visitor noting the posted list of the town's habitual drunkards mistook it for a roster of eligible voters. It was that long. Even more revealing as an example of intemperance was a bill covering the expenses for the festivities that attended the installation of the Reverend John Cornell as minister of the Presbyterian church in Allentown, New Jersey, in 1800. As cited by J. C. Furnas in his book *The Life and Times of the Late Demon Rum*, the bill included the following items: "Four large bowls of punch, a pint of brandy, one 'go' of grog, two bottles of wine, three and a half bottles of beer."

For the average colonist—and this included men, women, and children—the day began with a morning dose of spirits. This original "eye-opener" reflected the belief that such an alcoholic jolt was necessary to set the system going after the stagnation of sleep. The blood, it was believed, settled in the extremities during the night's sleep and had to be routed out by alcoholic stimulation. This morning jolt was also prophylactic in nature, since only alcohol could ward off the chills and fevers of the prevalent malaria which afflicted the colonists. Then the imbibing continued at regular intervals throughout the day until a final nightcap was downed to propel the drinker into sleep.

New England farmers at harvesttime customarily set a jug of rum at the edge of the hayfield where each mower took a swig every time he came around. This was the prescribed method for keeping up one's strength. Ships allotted a considerable portion of cargo space for barrels of beer and rum because a sailor expected no less than a quart of beer and pint of rum a day to keep him fit for his arduous tasks. Sailors believed firmly that only alcohol could ward off scurvy.

In Portland, Maine, the custom of "rum breaks" was so well established that the city hall bell was rung daily at 11 A.M. and again at 4 P.M. At these times all work stopped in the shipyards, shops, and factories, while all hands downed their cup of rum—provided at the bosses' expense, of course. In the hat and tailoring shops of Danbury, Connecticut, a new journeyman upon completing his apprenticeship was expected to buy drinks for all his shopmates to "pay his footing." A newly completed coat or suit called for "sponging" by the same method.

Nor was this liquid fortification reserved for only farmers and workingmen. Harvard College in Boston constructed a brewery soon after the school was opened to provide beer for students who were not expected to apply themselves to their studies without liquid lubricant. Clerks in banks and stores were also provided with the necessary rations of spirits.

In New England, wine and cider were supplied at public expense for the funerals of paupers. Proper respect for the dead demanded a liquid sendoff. The more affluent deceased, of course, were bidden farewell more generously. The company mourning an eminent Boston widow in 1678 consumed some fifty gallons of choice Madeira wine in their grief.

Religious tippling was not confined to funerals. Indeed, every religious occasion from christenings to weddings, convocations, synods, revival meetings, and the installations of new pastors were scenes of fervent celebration. The typical colonial clergyman making rounds of pastoral calls often returned home the worse for wear. Each household visited was expected to offer him a drink, and the pastor was expected to drink it.

An open jug of rum from which shoppers could draw a sustaining snort to help dispel the fatigue of shopping was commonly provided by groceries, hardware stores, and other retail establishments. And, of course, no man was expected to sit down in a barber's chair without first being fortified with strong spirits. When election time rolled around, all stops were removed. Candidates vied with each other in the largess of their liquid donations, and any man who was able to walk to the polling place in a straight line was suspected of treason.

Horace Greeley, famed editor of the New York *Tribune* and staunch abolitionist, as well as an advocate of temperance, in writing about his childhood in Derry, New Hampshire, recalled the role of apple cider in the rural life of New England. After the harvest in the fall, the Greeley family regularly put up some 100 barrels of cider as the year's supply.

Anyone who dropped in, Greeley wrote, "had his glass filled again and again until everybody was as full as he could hold . . . whole families died drunkards and vagabond paupers from the impetus first given by cider-swilling in their rural homes."

This cider, it must be emphasized, had little resemblance to the apple juice people drink today. This was a bubbling, fermented beverage with an alcoholic content equal to that of the strongest wines.

America, or so it would appear from these early accounts, floated on alcohol. It is not surprising, then, that this popular commodity played a central role in the economic development of the nation. Rum and whiskey were the principal items in trade with the Indians and as such were central to the lucrative fur trade—not to mention the fact that these spirits were also one of the most potent instruments in the destruction of Indian tribal life. Benjamin Franklin commented on this role in his *Autobiography* in a reference that we would consider brutal today, but was commonplace at the time: ". . . if it be the design of Providence to extirpate these savages in order to make room for the cultivators of the earth, it seems not improbable that rum may be the appointed means. . . ."

Farmers in Pennsylvania, Maryland, and Virginia depended on distilling as the most practical and profitable method of transporting a rye crop to market. For many small farmers whiskey was the main cash crop that they depended on to enable them to purchase necessities. The Whiskey Rebellion that occurred soon after the Revolution revealed the importance these farmers attached to this commodity.

In New England a most profitable and influential mercantile venture was organized around rum. This was the infamous Triangular Trade: Rum, distilled from molasses in New

England refineries, was shipped to Africa, where the potent liquid was traded for slaves. The slaves were then transported to the West Indies, where they were bartered for molasses. In the final leg of the triangle, the molasses was returned to New England, where it was distilled into rum as the beginning of a new cycle.

Great fortunes were founded on this inhuman trade, and these fortunes were at the basis, in many cases, of a New England aristocracy which was to have so strong an influence on the future history of the United States. The trade also established a maritime tradition in New England, along with a financial supremacy for the Northeast that continues to this day. In the South, as we shall see in Chapter 4, another drug—tobacco—played a similar role in the economy of that area. Odd that drugs should have played so important a role in the development of the United States. We can safely say that without the economic impetus provided by these two drugs, American history would have been vastly different.

These accounts of the drinking habits of our forefathers may seem exaggerated to the modern reader, but only a drinking problem of monstrous proportion could have spurred the next episode in the history of alcohol in America. Indeed, the great temperance crusades that rocked the nation throughout the nineteenth century and culminated in the passage of the Volstead Act in 1919 can be explained only in terms of a reaction to a real and pressing evil. In a heroic effort, American reformers sought to change the drug habit of a nation at first through persuasion and finally through law and legislation.

Before the temperance movement changed the national attitude, there was no social onus attached to drinking. Drunkenness, of course, was decried; but it was generally tolerated, and all men were expected to stagger home periodically in an alcoholic daze. Alcohol was accepted on all levels of society. The fact that a young Quaker could stand up at a meeting in colonial Philadelphia shortly before the Revolution and complain that he "was oppressed with the smell of rum from the breaths of those who sat around him" reveals how much that attitude has changed. Today the very idea of Quakers with rum on their breaths at a Sunday meeting is unthinkable.

For a hundred years, American reformers thundered against the evils of Demon Rum. War had been declared, and no holds were barred. Every resource of persuasion and coercion was enlisted in the cause. In their battle, the temperance forces developed techniques and methods of mass action that are still used. They organized societies, convened meetings; they held colorful torchlight parades in which massed ranks chanted antialcohol slogans; they composed songs and sang them; they wrote books and pamphlets; they staged propagandistic plays, of which *Ten Nights in a Barroom* was the most famous; and even the popular *McGuffey's Reader* joined the cause and young scholars practiced their reading with such elevating lines as:

> O, water for me! Bright water for me
> And wine for the tremulous debauchee. . . .

At its start, this campaign was purely moral in nature. Temperance leaders sought to persuade people to abstain from drink voluntarily. The evils of alcohol were forcefully described in lectures, sermons, street-corner talks, and pamphlets that were distributed everywhere. Although these methods were successful, for the most part, and the temperance forces grew steadily across the nation, this very success probably spurred the rum fighters to more vigorous action.

In the city of Syracuse, New York, in the year 1853, a certain Mrs. Margaret Freeland unwittingly, perhaps, devised a tactic that was to become increasingly important in the temperance battle. Her husband had been in the habit of stopping off at a local saloon for liquid refreshment before returning home from work. He was, it seemed, so devoted a customer that his excesses had habitually required the interference of the law. Mrs. Freeland had begged the saloonkeeper to stop selling to her husband on numerous occasions. His refusals finally prompted her to take a more direct course of action.

Mrs. Freeland, apparently a woman of robust constitution, procured a heavy wooden staff with which she battered down the door of the saloon. She then proceeded to smash all the bottles and glasses within club's reach. The hapless saloonkeeper, according to contemporary reports, also came within range of Mrs. Freeland's weapon and suffered a severe, though nonfatal concussion. Mrs. Freeland was, of course, arrested for her troubles. Her cause, however, came to the attention of the local temperance people, who procured counsel for her and made something of a celebrity of the woman. The saloonkeeper, frightened perhaps by the notoriety, withdrew charges despite the painful bump on his head.

The actions of Mrs. Freeland received nationwide publicity and were soon emulated in similar incidents. Mrs. Freeland had acted alone on impulse. Those who were to follow in her footsteps, however, decided wisely that there is strength in numbers and purpose in organization. Bands of women began to gather throughout the country to do battle directly with the stubborn Demon Rum. This tactic became so popular in the temperance movement that it seemed that no saloon in the country was safe from rampaging women. Ax-wielding Carry

Nation, of course, became the new symbol of temperance warriors.

Horace Greeley, himself a prohibitionist, noting this new development, predicted in an editorial he wrote in the *Tribune* that: "The next war in this country will be between women and whiskey, and though there will not be much blood shed rum will flow freely in the gutters."

Finally, the temperance forces, which came to represent a majority opinion in America, turned to politics. The climax of this effort came with the passage of the Volstead Act in 1919. The battle had been won. The forces of good had triumphed over those of evil. Henceforth, Demon Rum with all his attendant ills would be banished from the nation.

Alas, the triumph came too late. Momentous social changes had taken place in the interim, changes that would sweep aside all the good intentions and purposes of prohibition. A world war had intervened and altered the character of the United States irrevocably.

Before that war, in 1914, America was a large country, and no one doubted that it was rich. Blessed with almost unlimited natural resources, having one of the largest and richest belts of fertile farmland in the world, protected from European intrigues by an ocean, boasting a vigorous and growing population, America had no limits to its potential. Yet in 1914 this potential was barely making itself felt upon the international scene. America was a provincial country far from the seats of power. London was the financial capital of the world, and Paris was the cultural center. Study in a German university was a must for any ambitious young American who hoped to make a mark in medicine, philosophy, or science.

The United States was primarily a rural, agricultural nation with the bulk of its population living on farms or in small towns. Although the seeds of a great industrial capacity had been sown, this factor was still of only minor international significance. Our technical know-how was not highly considered, and our popular culture—music, movies, dance—had not yet Americanized the leisure life of the world.

American financiers, except when they had to borrow money abroad, were totally involved with domestic affairs. At this time the United States was a debtor nation whose industrial expansion was financed in large part by European banks. In 1914, this debt totaled some $7 billion—a huge figure, but even larger when calculated against the buying power of the 1914 dollar when a pound of the finest steak cost 6 cents and a good pair of work boots could be bought for 95 cents.

World War I changed the position of America in world affairs overnight. For one thing, this was the most destructive and expensive war the world had known till that time. It consumed men and materials on a scale that dwarfed all earlier conflicts. American business found itself with an unlimited and profitable market for everything it could produce. Steel and dynamite, potatoes and cotton, boots and trucks were consumed or destroyed on the battlefields of Europe as fast as we could deliver them. In the three years between 1914 and 1917, America paid off its debt to Europe and for the first time in its history became a creditor rather than a debtor nation.

To meet the demands made by this war—which America itself entered in 1917—our industry and agriculture performed miracles of expansion. In American factories the machines never stopped, and every hand worked overtime. Every farmer cultivated all the land he could manage, and then some, while accumulated capital grew steadily in the banks and counting-houses.

As for the war itself, it had no great physical effect on America. No bombs fell on our cities, and no battle was waged on our soil. We suffered heavy casualties—some 126,000 servicemen died in the war—but neither our military nor our economic resources had been in any way overburdened.

Our economy had outfitted an enormous army from scratch and kept it lavishly provisioned and equipped. We had supplied the Allies with unheard-of quantities of food, clothing, metal, fuels, weapons, and ammunition. We had built billions of dollars' worth of airplanes, tanks, and trucks and had feverishly constructed the largest navy in the world.

Then, after the Armistice, America turned its greatly expanded industrial and agricultural capacity to the pursuits of peace. It embarked on a decade of prosperity and expansion that dazzled the world. America had arrived. We were the richest, freest, strongest, most productive society the world had ever seen, a newly emerged center of power that all the world had to recognize.

In this atmosphere of newly won success and wealth, in the unfamiliar role of world power, Prohibition foundered. It was somehow incongruous that in Washington, D.C., visiting dignitaries could not be entertained with so much as a glass of wine. In this heady atmosphere, which affected the entire nation, the high moral purposes of Prohibition were doomed.

No one could deny the good intentions and moral fervor that stood behind the Prohibition laws, and as such they represented the last gasp of a tradition that enjoyed a brief moment of dominance in America—a tradition that in retrospect becomes enormously appealing. But, as was soon made painfully clear, that tradition was moribund and withering away almost as soon as it had borne fruit. From the very beginnings of Prohibition it was evident that the moral life of a nation was impossible to regulate by law.

People continued to buy and sell liquor even though they were aware that to do so was a crime. The law was simply ignored. Bootlegging, the illegal manufacture and smuggling of liquor, became a national industry on a scale that presupposed the wholesale corruption of police and government officials. Illegal saloons and cabarets where liquor was sold flourished throughout the country in open defiance of the law.

Prohibition had split both major parties as it did the nation and became the most controversial and talked-about issue in politics. In the face of the unprecedented prosperity of the 1920's, a subtle change occurred in the outlook of the nation. Breaking the law became a fascinating game, and hardly anyone considered the consequences—the widespread corruption of the police, the establishment and growth to power of underworld empires. In the popular mind the drys became identified with country preachers, farmers, old maids, and professional killjoys. The wets became handsome young men and pretty girls. They were jolly good fellows and sports; they were dashing rumrunners and gallant police officers who acted out an exciting charade.

Yet Prohibition had been a noble experiment. In its time it represented the most progressive and liberal force in American politics. It attracted some of the finest people this nation has produced to its cause. Abraham Lincoln, Walt Whitman, Susan B. Anthony, Henry Ward Beecher, Horace Greeley, Thoreau, Emerson, and Longfellow were among the luminous lights that lent their influence and energy to the good cause.

These same people, it must be remembered, were also in the forefront of the battle for many other reforms and social innovations whose adoption did so much to alleviate and temper the harsher aspects of early American society. Along with Demon Rum, they did honorable battle against slavery, child labor, the brutal treatment of the American Indians; they instituted prison reforms, helped reorganize the public schools, and demanded humane treatment for mental patients.

The temperance movement also saw the beginning of agitation for Women's Liberation. For the first time in American history, women organized and came together to attempt to influence their own lives. Women bore the brunt of the enormous cost of alcoholism, and they led in the fight to abolish this evil. Women's suffrage, as just one advance, was directly related to the temperance movement, and today's Women's Liberation drive had its beginning in meetings where women came together to see what they might do to stop a deadly evil.

Those who participated in the temperance struggle had courage. In a society that was, in many respects, drunken, cruel, and brutal they stood up and spoke out for sobriety and humanity. They also had vision—of a society perfected, of a noble republic where slavery, poverty, drunkenness, cruelty, and injustice would be abolished. They believed fervently in the perfectibility of man and tried to translate this belief into practice.

By the time Prohibition had become the law of the land it was already obsolete, outmoded. To the world at large and to many Americans it was nothing more than an old-fashioned, unrealistic appeal to an idealism that had never really existed.

Prohibitionists were jokes of the vaudeville stage, their high moral purpose and dream of a perfect society a laughable delusion.

Prohibition died on December 5, 1933. This was the legal date of the demise. In fact, however, the people themselves, without benefit of Congress or courts, had repealed the law almost as soon as it was passed. For fourteen years the law was ignored, broken, and disregarded. In acting to ratify the Twenty-first Amendment, Congress was merely confirming what everyone in the country had known as a fact for years.

Yet the great temperance crusades left a mark that still colors our attitudes toward alcohol. Few of us, even to this day, are able to take even a small social drink without a twinge of conscience. They left us the image of the alcoholic as skid-row derelict—as the man who has forsaken his humanity to the lures of the bottle. Echoes of that crusade continue to act as a brake on our drinking habits.

Today alcohol is no longer the frightening demon portrayed by the prohibitionists. It is an accepted part of life that supports an important industry whose revenues are indispensable to the function of government. As a social stimulant alcohol continues to play an important role in our leisure life. What party or celebration is complete without the enlivening presence of the old demon?

Alas, it also remains a problem. Alcoholism is by far the most serious and costly addictive disease in the nation. For too many people it remains the "gift of the devil" that makes of their lives a living hell. Still, the rate of alcoholism in America appears to be stabilized. It has remained at the same figure of 3 to 4 percent of the population for the past thirty years—it also remains far below the percentage figures of seventy years ago, when an estimated 11 percent were so afflicted.

Most of us today recognize alcoholism as a disease, a sickness that afflicts some of us much as diabetes or rheumatism does. Our treatment of alcoholics has become much more humane and understanding. Our insights into the dynamics and causes of alcoholism promise to reduce further the rate of occurrence of this disease. In short, we are learning to live with our national drug.

And live with it we must. History has shown how deeply entrenched alcohol is in our psyches. We no longer believe we can eradicate it by government edict, nor do we feel that eradication is necessary. In moderation, alcohol is one of the pleasures of life, a pleasure that will be with us as far into the future as we can see.

Cheers!

4. TOBACCO: THE GOLDEN WEED

IF ALCOHOL was the great contribution of Europe to the drug spectrum of the world, then tobacco is the gift of America. Both the plant and the drug were unknown in Europe, Asia, or Africa before Columbus. Tobacco grew only in North and South America, where it was cultivated wherever the hardy plant could grow. The practice of smoking the leaves of the plant either in a rolled-up wad of leaves or stuffed into the bowl of a pipe was common among all the people of the Western Hemisphere with the exception of the Eskimos who lived in the far reaches of the Arctic.

The first inkling that Europeans had about the existence of this interesting plant and drug came when Columbus and members of his crew noticed a strange practice among the people whom they found in the New World. Many of them carried wads of rolled leaves which they set on fire and left to smolder. They then placed the unlit ends into their mouths and sucked vigorously, inhaling the smoke from the smoldering leaves into their lungs.

This amazing practice appeared to be common among these

74

heathen people. Men, women, and children indulged in the practice with what seemed to be great satisfaction. Some had small pipes with a bowl attached to one end. This bowl would be filled with the same kind of leaves, set on fire, and left to smolder. The smoke produced was breathed in through the other end of the tube and drawn into the lungs. Later European explorers discovered that besides smoking these leaves, the Indians chewed them and sniffed a finely ground powder by holding a pinch to the nostrils and ingesting it with a quick intake of breath.

One of the principal reasons for the popularity of tobacco among the Indians was their belief in the medicinal properties of the leaf. According to the Indians, tobacco prevented fevers and bronchial diseases and was an indispensable aid in the treatment of a variety of ailments. In addition, they found that the smoking of tobacco had a soothing effect on the nerves and temper. Thus, the smoking of a peace pipe was part of the ritual that accompanied all intertribal conferences and meetings. Smoldering pipes and rolled-up wads of tobacco leaves were undoubtedly offered to Columbus and members of his crew when they set foot upon the New World.

Some probably gagged on the first puff, a few might even have become violently ill, but many enjoyed it and tried another and then another. We know that when Columbus returned to Spain, one of the treasures he brought back was tobacco and its seeds. We also know that many of his crew members had learned to smoke and had made provision for the satisfaction of this new habit.

Actually, as we have seen, the people of the New World had developed many psychedelic and hallucinogenic drugs. The use of these substances was central to both their religious and their social lives. Tobacco, however, was the one New World

75

drug that gained universal acceptance in the shortest span of time. Within fifty years of the discovery of America by Columbus, tobacco had reached into practically every corner of the globe!

No other drug in history spread across the world so quickly and so thoroughly. Even more amazing, this dissemination occurred at a time of sailing ships and horse-drawn wagons, when there were no means of rapid communication—no radio, telegraph, or telephone. It seemed almost as if the world had been waiting for this aromatic leaf and, more important perhaps, this novel method of ingestion through inhalation of smoke.

At the time, this rapid dissemination appeared to be a bewildering phenomenon. Many saw in it the hand of the devil! Today, however, we can understand some of the reasons for this rapid acceptance of tobacco. We know that nicotine, the principal active ingredient in tobacco, is a highly addicting drug. Indeed, it is probably the most readily addictive substance known. *Statistical studies show that three cigarettes smoked in adolescence is sufficient in more than 80 percent of all cases to addict the smoker for the rest of his life!*

What this means is that out of every 100 adolescents who smoke at least three cigarettes, 80 will become regular smokers. More statistics: out of these 80 smokers, *90 percent* will smoke more than fifteen cigarettes per day—or one cigarette every waking hour! Can we imagine what a catastrophe it would be if 80 percent of all people who tried three drinks in their youth became alcoholics?

Besides the addictive property of nicotine, smoking provides compelling satisfactions of a purely psychological nature. One, of course, is the oral satisfaction of clutching a pipe, cigar, or cigarette in the lips, sucking and chewing on the stem, and using the mouth in the act of ingestion. Another is the manipulative action of the fingers and hands in lighting and smoking the pipe, cigar, or cigarette/In Turkey, Greece, China, India, and other Eastern countries worry beads have been developed to satisfy this craving. Throughout the East men commonly finger a string of beads held in the hand while transacting business, talking among themselves, or simply while walking or sitting alone. Smoking provides an effective substitute.

Smoking is also one of the most efficient techniques for ingesting a drug that we know. Blood is oxygenated in the lungs before being pumped through the rest of the body. A drug inhaled as smoke or a vapor into the lungs is picked up by the blood along with oxygen with little loss of either volume or potency. An orally administered dose must pass through the stomach and intestines where it is affected by gastric juices before it can enter the bloodstream. Only direct injection into a vein is a more efficient means of ingesting a drug than smoking.

Finally, there is another unique property of nicotine as a drug. It is the most chameleonlike of all mind-altering substances—though most drugs share this quality to a limited degree—eliciting the effects the user desires at any particlar moment. Nicotine acts as a stimulant, a tranquilizer, a relaxant, or a depressant according to the need of the user! Thus, we find that people smoke after great exertion or tension to relax them; before an ordeal, be it a test in school or an important interview for a job, as a stimulant; at the end of a busy day as a most effective tranquilizer; at times of great joy or sorrow to enhance or subdue these emotions. In short, nicotine acts in response to situational demands—no matter what they may be.

It is not surprising, then, that the practice of smoking tobacco quickly found adherents. Sailors, of course, who visited the New World were the principal disseminators of this new drug. They brought tobacco to Spain and introduced it to sailors from other nations. Thus when Magellan began his epic circumnavigation of the world in September, 1519, a good percentage of the crew—which represented at least nine European and African nationalities, including one Englishman, a master gunner named Andrews—had already been introduced to tobacco.

Not only did members of Magellan's crew smoke tobacco, but in order to ensure an adequate supply, they carried ample stores of both the leaf and the seed. On their circumnavigation, these seeds were planted wherever no tobacco grew in order to assure a supply should they sail to those parts again. In this way, tobacco was introduced to Guam in the Marianas Islands in the Pacific; to the Philippine Islands; to India; to China; and to Africa. In short, wherever the ships of Magellan's fleet touched shore, there the sailors planted the seeds they carried and there they introduced this compelling New World drug.

At the same time, tobacco was being introduced to the rest of Europe. Tobacco was smoked in France in 1540, England in 1550, Holland in 1550, Italy soon after. Jean Nicot, French ambassador at Lisbon in the mid-sixteenth century, after whom the *Nicotiana* plant is named, sent seeds of the tobacco plant to Catherine de Médicis, then Regent of France.

In the beginning, tobacco was looked on as an exotic novelty from the New World. It was enormously expensive, and its use was limited to only the wealthiest. But then it was quickly realized that this amazing leaf had an almost unlimited market potential. Large-scale cultivation of the plant was soon instituted to supply this need. The first commercial tobacco plantation was organized on the island of Santo Domingo in 1528, and large-scale cultivation soon spread to all the islands of the Caribbean and into Mexico and South America. The first commercial tobacco plantation in North America was established in the Jamestown, Virginia, colony by John Rolfe in 1612. Within twenty-five years, tobacco became the principal export of the English colonies of North America, and was grown from New England to the Carolinas.

What was a novelty for the rich soon became a necessity for all. By 1610 English moralists were complaining that the compulsion for tobacco was the financial ruin of "young noblemen," as well as commoners. Sir Francis Bacon noted that "the use of tobacco is growing greatly and conquers men with a certain secret pleasure." Some 7,000 tobacco shops were serving London in the year 1614.

So rapid was the spread of the tobacco habit and so compelling was the need for the leaf that authorities in practically every country where it was introduced sought to ban the habit. Indeed, even the august Catholic Church joined in the battle to stop the spread of the pernicious weed. In 1642 Pope Urban VIII issued a formal bull condemning the use of tobacco in any form—a new sin had appeared to bedevil mankind from the New World! In 1650 Pope Innocent X reiterated the church's stand against the noxious drug. Both edicts failed to stop the practice and people continued to smoke—even at the risk of their immortal souls!

Secular rulers confined themselves to the earthy realm, and their prohibitions were enforced by corporal threat. In Russia, Czar Michael Fedorovich Romanov—the first of this dynasty —punished smokers by cutting off their noses, beating the soles of their bare feet bloody in the painful bastinado, or simply scourging them with the weighted knout. These emphatic enforcements of the czar's prohibition laws were about as successful as the Pope's bans. In both cases, people kept right on smoking. The threat of neither bodily nor spiritual disaster could constrain them.

In Turkey the rulers were not inhibited by Christian scruple—though they agreed on the necessity of preventing the vice of tobacco smoking. Sultan Murad IV in a royal decree issued in 1633 decreed a colorful death for anyone caught smoking. The hapless Turkish smoker lived under threat of death by hanging, beheading, quartering between four strong horses, or being incarcerated in a public cage without food or water (or tobacco, of course) until death intervened. When the sultan did not impose the death penalty, he merely had the smoker's hands and legs crushed between great stones as an object lesson.

Tobacco was introduced into Japan by Portuguese seamen in 1542. Within twenty years the habit had spread throughout all the Japanese islands, and the first edict against the drug was decreed in 1590, followed by sterner measures in a law enacted in 1603. The Japanese, apparently a gentler people than either Russians or Turks, merely confiscated a smoker's property. Those without property were jailed.

The English, more mercantile, if not more humane than Russians, Turks, Japanese, or Popes, recognized the financial possibilities of tobacco. Here was a substance whose use was almost impossible to stop once a user became accustomed to its peculiar effects. Instead of prohibiting the use of this mysterious leaf, the English *taxed it!* Almost immediately, the treasury had a new, significant source of revenue that was given up by tobacco users with a minimum of complaint.

Such financial success could not be hidden for long, and

other nations in Europe followed suit. Tobacco would no longer be prohibited—it would be taxed. In time, Turks and Japanese followed suit. With this new orientation, the use of tobacco continued to grow—possibly at a faster pace than it would have otherwise, but we cannot be sure. This growth created additional demand, and this demand was met, in great part, by production on New World plantations.

By the beginning of the eighteenth century tobacco was the principal export of the English colonies in North America. Great plantations were organized for its cultivation, and a steady stream of ships carried tobacco from Virginia, the Carolinas, Maryland, Pennsylvania, and New Jersey to England. Slavery was introduced into the colonies to provide the labor necessary for this cultivation, and tobacco became one of the basic economic factors in the growth of the New World.

Meanwhile, in the rest of Europe and the world, attitudes toward tobacco were undergoing a subtle change. The original wave of harsh repression which was the initial reaction of authority to the new drug gave way to acceptance and even, in many cases, to advocacy of tobacco. Medicinal qualities were soon discovered in tobacco smoke and in snuff, and physicians all over Europe were prescribing both smoking and sniffing as beneficial in many ailments. During this period, also, the use of tobacco continued to spread. Actually, there is no case on record where a people who have become accustomed to the use of tobacco have given up the practice.

In time, regional strains of tobacco developed in various parts of the world. In Turkey, for example, a strain called latakia, a mild aromatic type of leaf, developed and has become one of the important tobaccos of world commerce. The most noted tobacco-growing area in the world, at least as far as cigars are concerned, is the Vuelta Abajo region in the province of Pinar del Río in western Cuba, where most of the fine wrapper leaf for Havana cigars is produced. Apparently, the agricultural conditions in this part of Cuba are ideal for the growing of tobacco leaf. Although the seed has been transplanted to tobacco-growing areas throughout the world, the fragrance of the Havana leaf has never been reproduced in another soil.

Throughout the nineteenth century tobacco continued to grow in importance as an agricultural commodity. By now the practice of taking nicotine—by smoking, chewing, or sniffing —was just about universal. Everybody, it seemed, regardless of race, creed, or national origin, had a penchant for tobacco. During this period the worldwide distribution of tobacco had become so organized that it was generally made available wherever people wanted to buy it, much like wheat, rice, or potatoes.

Before 1850 plug or chewing tobacco and snuff were the most popular form of tobacco in the United States. A little more than half the annual production was marketed in these forms with the remainder smoked in pipes and cigars. Cigarettes, though smoked by the Indians when Columbus first arrived, did not become popular until the twentieth century.

Two developments spurred the popularity of cigarettes to the dominant position in the industry that they now command. One was the development in 1864 of a strain of tobacco called white burley. This proved to be a mild, aromatic leaf that was ideal for cigarette smoking. The strain was first noticed by an Ohio farmer named George Webb who found a few plants that seemed to be deficient in color among his tobacco plants.

Webb isolated the seeds from these plants which became the

basis for this important strain. When cured, the light-colored leaf turned pale yellow and had a flexible, porous texture. The smoke was mild and pleasant to the taste. The variety has since been improved by selective breeding and is now widely grown. It remains the primary tobacco for cigarettes.

The second factor was the development of a practical machine for rolling cigarettes patented in 1880 by James A. Bonsack. Before the Bonsack machine, cigarettes were rolled by hand—an expensive operation despite the low, sweatshop wages paid hand rollers. The machine did the work of more than fifty hand rollers, producing about 100,000 cigarettes in eight hours. It reduced the cost of manufacture more than tenfold and production of cigarettes increased from about 500,000,000 in 1880 to 1 billion in 1885 and 4 billion in 1895.

It appeared as though cigarettes were the ideal form for the marketing of tobacco. Production increased steadily in a steep rise that continues to this day. Five billion cigarettes were manufactured in 1900, and almost 600 billion were sold in 1971. Today cigarettes represent 85 percent of all tobacco sold in America. This growth has continued steadily despite depressions, wars, and social upheaval. Today the tobacco industry is one of the mainstays of the American economy, upon which the American public spends almost $11 billion annually!

From a pharmacological point of view, this switch in preference is readily explained. Cigarette smokers can inhale the milder smoke from the burley deep into their lungs—most pipe and cigar smokers do not inhale—and thus receive their nicotine dose in a more efficient manner. Actually, the very size of the cigarette seems admirably adapted to the preferred dosage of the drug.

From a medical point of view, however, this switch has been

disastrous. The problem here is that when the smoker inhales in order to take his dose of nicotine, he also takes a lungful of what have proved to be deadly by-products of tobacco smoke. Parallel to the upward-rising curve of cigarette consumption has been the equally dramatic rise in the incidence of lung cancer. In 1900 lung cancer was a rare disease. Fewer than 1,000 people died of this malady in that year. In 1973 some 80,000 deaths were attributed to lung cancer!

The idea that smoking is detrimental to health is actually almost as old as the use of tobacco itself. It was almost immediately obvious that people who smoked were prone to lung disease, whether chronic coughing, bronchitis, or emphysema. Indeed, health consideration played a primary role in the original attempts to prohibit tobacco.

The first published medical report on the subject, however, was not issued until 1859. Physicians in a hospital in Montpellier, France, noted that sixty-eight patients who suffered cancer of the lips, tongue, throat, or other parts of the mouth all used tobacco. Sixty-six of them smoked a then popular short-stemmed pipe. Following the release of the report, this type of pipe fell out of favor.

Not much further attention was paid to the relationship between smoking and health until cigarette smoking became increasingly popular following World War I. Then, in country after country where cigarette smoking was heavy, medical reports showed an alarming increase in lung cancer, incidence of emphysema, and heart disease. The tobacco industry, however, had grown enormously in the interim. It involved billions of dollars, employed hundreds of thousands of people, and commanded corresponding political influence. The reports on the health hazards of smoking were played down and did not receive wide publicity or coverage in the mass media.

But medical evidence kept mounting until it could no longer be ignored. In 1954 the American Cancer Society reported, after a three-year statistical study, that death rates were higher for smokers than they were for nonsmokers at every age level. A man between forty-five and fifty-four years of age who had smoked steadily since his teens was three times more likely to die than the man, in the same age bracket, who did not smoke.

An independently conducted study in England came to the same conclusion. Cigarette smoking was killing people. The evidence was clear and unmistakable. A significant response to these reports, which were publicized, was felt almost immediately. In the fall of 1954, when the reports were made public, there was a measurable drop in the consumption of cigarettes. But then came a more ominous development. Within two months, after the initial reaction had subsided somewhat, the trend reversed itself. Sales of cigarettes soared. The small losses were wiped out, and new sales records were established every year.

People did not stop smoking! Surveys revealed that smokers were aware of the dangers, but they kept right on puffing away at their cigarettes. Between 1954 and 1964 consumption of cigarettes rose stubbornly year by year. It was as though there never had been an American Cancer Society report. Sales did not reflect any concern on the part of American smokers.

Finally, in 1964 the Surgeon General of the United States was compelled to intervene. Lung cancer had developed into an epidemic killer with some 64,000 deaths reported in 1963! *Ninety-seven percent of the victims were heavy cigarette smokers.* The danger, however, did not stop there. In addition to lung cancer, cigarette smoking was found to be a factor in numerous other dangerous diseases, including emphysema, heart disease, and a variety of circulatory disorders.

In January, 1964, the Surgeon General's report on the hazards of cigarette smoking was released and received wide coverage and publicity. Manufacturers were compelled to print a warning on every pack of cigarettes and, later, on all advertisements to the effect that smoking was dangerous to the health. Tobacco, the "Golden Weed" of the Americas, appeared to have reached its demise. Now that the proof of the danger was indisputable, no one would voluntarily continue to smoke.

For a time—a very brief time, as it turned out—it seemed that the Surgeon General's warning would be heeded. All over the country cigarette sales dropped significantly. The number of taxed cigarette packages was reduced about 20 percent in the month of February, 1964. This was a nationwide decline and the first such decline registered in the history of cigarette smoking in America.

If the tobacco companies and those who depended on the industry for their livelihood were put into a panic, health authorities congratulated themselves on their timely intervention. At this rate, it was believed, cigarette smoking might disappear before the end of the year or at least shrink to the point where it would no longer be a major health hazard.

Unfortunately, the authorities did not allow for the compulsive power of drug addiction. Within two months after the report was issued, and after the first flurry of excitement subsided, cigarette sales were back to normal. In fact, consumption resumed its steady increase. The sales figures tell the story very well:

1963	523.9 billion cigarettes smoked		
1964	511.2	"	"	"
1965	528.7	"	"	"
1966	541.2	"	"	"
1967	549.2	"	"	"

In 1968 there was a slight drop in cigarette consumption to 545.6 billion, but the figure has since climbed steadily. In 1970, for example, 542 billion cigarettes were smoked, and in 1973 sales had climbed to 600 billion. This rise occurred despite unprecedented government and health agency attempts to curb the habit. Taxes on cigarettes were raised 40 percent; cigarette advertising was prohibited on television; warnings had to be more prominently displayed on all cigarette packs and advertisements.

Nothing helped. Smokers kept right on buying cigarettes at the same astronomical level. As far as the tobacco companies were concerned, their financial position was improved, if anything. They no longer spent millions of dollars on television advertisements. Actually, a similar experience in Italy, where all cigarette advertising was banned, had similar results. Tobacco sales were in no way affected by the prohibition!

Cigarette smoking had been considered no more than a particularly pernicious habit. We all knew that it was a difficult habit to control, but no one considered tobacco a *real* drug. Our experience with smoking in relationship to its health hazards has unquestionably refuted this concept. Smokers are addicted, and they may be addicted to the most powerfully compulsive substance we know.

Recent tests indicate that people smoke, chew, or sniff tobacco primarily for the nicotine content. It is not a question of doing something with your hands or an ingrained ritual of reaching for a cigarette, putting it to your lips, and lighting it—though these are, of course, additional elements in this powerful addiction. Nicotine is what the addict craves, and it makes little difference to him how he receives his dose.

All addiction seems to be similar in many respects. One, of course, is in the power of the compulsion. Another becomes quite obvious when the rates or recidivism for heroin addicts, alcoholics, and tobacco smokers are compared. In each case, projection on a graph appears almost identical. Within a period of five years, 90 percent or more have resumed their habits.

Still, it would seem impossible to compare tobacco addiction with heroin addiction. There are less than one-tenth the number of heroin addicts as there are smokers, and there is no comparison between the social damage done by heroin and tobacco. True, but this is primarily because tobacco is readily available while heroin is illegal and can be purchased only through illegal sources. As we shall see in Chapter 6, the narcotics addict who is supplied with the drug is not very different from everyone else.

Most cigarette smokers have never experienced a real shortage. When they have, the addictive quality of tobacco becomes more obvious. After World War II a significant shortage of cigarettes developed in Europe immediately after the fighting stopped. In these circumstances, smokers acted very much like heroin addicts or alcoholics. In order to get cigarettes, people stole, lied, and cheated and women prostituted themselves. In many cases, people reduced to a starvation-level diet traded food for cigarettes! Indeed, cigarettes became a substitute for money in the turmoil that followed that most destructive of all wars.

Actually, cigarette smoking, because it is so common, offers a convenient analogy to all drug addiction. Why do people smoke? Certainly, any smoker will tell you, the actual pleasure experienced from the practice is negligible. There is no high. There is only this powerful craving when smoking is stopped.

Heroin addicts describe a similar reaction to their drug. They do not get high, they do not feel any great ecstasy or physical pleasure. All they know is that when they do not take the drug, they suffer a powerful craving that must be relieved. They take drugs in order to feel *normal,* in order to be able to function. Cigarette smokers report the same feeling.

Indeed, cigarette smoking may be the more powerful addiction, as can be seen in reactions to Buerger's disease. This is a rare malady in which victims experience a reaction to nicotine that constricts the blood vessels to such a degree that circulation is impaired. Should a patient suffering from Buerger's disease continue smoking, gangrene can develop in the extremities, with amputation the only alternative.

Progress of this disease is virtually certain to stop if the patient stops smoking. In one reported case, a patient's arms and legs were amputated, but he continued smoking though he could no longer light or hold his cigarette! Obviously, there is something much more compulsive here than mere habit. Today we have similar confirmation of the power of nicotine addiction. In 1973 an estimated 80,000 people will die of lung cancer. We know that cigarette smoking is a primary cause. We also know that people will continue smoking—some even after they have been operated upon!

Is official prohibition the solution? Shall we ban the growing, import, manufacture, and possession of tobacco products? Certainly, there is more than enough justification for even so drastic a remedy. According to HEW estimates, some 250,000 to 350,000 people will die prematurely as a result of smoking in 1973. It has also been estimated that the smoker shortens his life expectancy by *ten years!* These, we must remember, are not wild accusations made by puritanical moralists and killjoys—they are the result of careful, conservative, scientific study.

In contrast, heroin addiction might appear to be benign. No more than 2,500 deaths, according to official estimates, will be caused by heroin addiction in the same year. At the same time, these 2,500 deaths will cause a furor of publicity, demands for reform, revenge, law enforcement, etc., etc., etc. The 350,000—let us be even more conservative than HEW and say 200,000—deaths attributed to cigarettes will cause hardly a stir. You explain the difference. The writer cannot.

Still, there seems little likelihood that cigarettes will be banned. Too many people smoke, and the industry is too firmly entrenched. Besides, prohibition would probably lead to conditions that are even worse. Imagine what would happen if 10,000,000 nicotine-starved addicts began to act up? The heroin situation would probably seem like a picnic in comparison.

If nothing else, cigarettes serve as a constant reminder of the compulsive power of drugs. The American Indians, who introduced so many mind-altering drugs, were aware of this power. Use of drugs in Indian society was carefully controlled by custom and tradition. Shamans recognized this power, and took carefully calculated steps to control it—even the pipe in which drugs were smoked was an object of sanctity and awe.

We can experience the same awe when we witness a cigarette smoker happily "walk a mile" for his . . . LUNG CANCER!

5. MARY JANE: THE DEVIL WEED

Logs were burning in the fireplace, sending tongues of flame dancing up the flue, the light reflected in the wood paneling of the darkened dining room. Six couples were gathered in front of the fire, seated about a large, round oaken table. All were in their late thirties and early forties, and all had growing, school-age children. Professional people for the most part, their number included teachers, lawyers, a doctor, an artist, a musician, and a writer. All were well, if casually, dressed, and only a mild hirsuteness evident in a few of the men betrayed anything of a bohemian tendency.

The room, bathed in the soft, flickering light from the fireplace, had "good vibes"—it breathed an air of warmth and familiarity. A bottle of wine was on the table, along with glasses and several trays that held grapes, oranges, apples, and pears. A hi-fi set in the adjoining room spun out the cool, subtle syncopations of a Miles Davis recording. There was laughter and talk in the room, though both were gentle, almost subdued.

An oddly shaped brass pipe engraved in a floral design and

small enough to hold comfortably in the hand was being passed around the table. It was a water pipe from India with white wine taking the place of water in the tank. As though celebrating a tribal ritual, each person in turn would draw on the pipe once or twice—inhaling the smoke deeply—and pass it along to the next person in the circle. Smoldering in the bowl were dried leaves and flowers of the hemp plant (*Cannabis sativa*) together with scrapings from a stick of what was said to be Iranian hashish—a more potent preparation of the resin of cannabis. The smoke filled the room with a characteristic sweet, pungent odor.

A casual observer in the room would have recognized no signs of depravity or even intoxication. The people in the room would appear normal. Their speech would not be slurred, they would not stagger, and their motor ability would seem in no way impaired. A medical examination would also show little irregularity. Blood pressure might rise slightly above normal; an increase in blood sugar level might be detected, and the basal metabolic rate might go up a little; in addition, some might experience a slight dryness in the mucous membranes and an increase in the frequency of urination. These effects, however, would be minimal and would require minute examinations to be detected.

Actually, the effects of cannabis, the drug being used by the people in this pleasant dining room, are generally subjective and internal. There is very little that shows in a physiological sense even to the most careful examiner. If they were asked about their subjective experience, their answers would have been vague: "Food tastes better," one might say. "Music sounds richer," another might add. "Colors become deeper and shapes more definite. . . . Ideas seem to occur more readily in the mind. . . . I feel light, as though my body had lost its weight. . . . Everything seems funny. . . . Everyone looks so beautiful." And some, if they were honest, would admit that they felt nothing at all, that they participated only to be part of the group.

In many respects this was a typical gathering of a particular stratum of American society. Variations of the scene could be repeated in similar homes across the country. Literally millions of Americans will recognize the special setting and understand the reasons for the presence of the wine, the fruit, the music, and the firelight. And even more millions will be aware that the twelve people gathered that evening for a night's social diversion were criminals—criminals who could have been arrested and subjected to long prison terms and heavy fines. They were knowingly committing a crime—a very serious one in the light of current laws.

What precisely was the crime?

The possession and smoking of the leaves, flowers, and resin of the hemp plant (*Cannabis sativa*).

Why is this a crime?

Primarily because of a law passed by the Congress of the United States in the year 1937.

Why was this legislation enacted?

To find an answer to this question, we must look back over the long, strange history of cannabis in the United States and the efforts of our government to regulate the morality and pleasures of its citizens—of you and me.

Cannabis sativa (call it hemp, marijuana, maryjane, tea, pot, grass, gage, bhang, kiff, ganja, muggles, reefers, or a thousand other regional and local names) is one of the oldest drugs known to man. Chinese physicians described the plant and some of its interesting properties 2,500 years before the birth of Christ. They prescribed it regularly as a remedy for "gout,

93

rheumatism, malaria, constipation, loss of appetite, melancholia and as an aid in childbirth." Chinese moralists, on the other hand, noting the mildly euphoric property of the drug, called cannabis "liberator of sin."

The ancient Hindu sages of India held another view. They called the plant "joy-giver, the heavenly-guide, and the soother of grief" and considered the hemp plant holy and indispensable to the religious life. The Hindu warrior caste, however, looked down upon cannabis and claimed its use led to slothful dreaming and cowardice.

In ancient Egypt the people who erected the pyramids soothed and fortified themselves with a tea brewed from the leaves and flowers of the plant. The Greeks of Homer's age were familiar with cannabis, and fierce Scythian warriors chewed on its leaves before going into battle—a practice that was apparently used by American warriors in Vietnam, to the consternation of military officials.

Traces of the leaves, flowers, and seeds of the plant were identified in a funerary urn that came from a burial site in Wilmersdorf, Germany. Dr. Hermann Busse, the archaeologist who made the discovery, dated the urn to the fifth century B.C., placing it in the Neolithic (New Stone Age) of central Europe. Cannabis was evidently placed in the urn to ease the passage of the deceased into the unknown, frightening land of the dead. It is the "Herb Pantagruelion" lauded by François Rabelais, fifteenth-century French satirist and natural scientist, for its medicinal, commercial, and intoxicating properties. It would appear that the leaves and resin of the hemp plant were used for their medicinal and pleasurable properties from the very beginnings of human history.

Certainly, cannabis itself is one of the most common plants in the world. It is cultivated and grows wild in a remarkably wide range of climatic and soil conditions. Stands of the hardy plant grow in the steaming rain forests of Africa and South America; it can be found growing in the arid highlands of Mexico and the Middle East; it grows in India and China; it can survive in the temperate zone as far north as Halifax, Canada, and Glasgow, Scotland; it grows lushly in the jungles of Indochina. Cannabis will flourish almost wherever a seed is planted in the earth.

As a drug, cannabis is ingested by smoking, drinking, or eating various preparations of the leaves, flowers, and resins of the plant. In America the preferred method of ingestion is by smoking. The manner in which the drug affects the body is understood only vaguely. What this means is that, like aspirin, we do not know how it works. The physiological effects of the drug are known to be manifestations of cerebral excitation, the impulses of this excitation being transmitted through the autonomic system. Those alterations in the functions of the organs that have been observed in controlled studies appear to be the result of the effects of the drug on the central nervous system. A direct action on the organs themselves has never been verified. One thing, however, is certain: Cannabis is not a narcotic even though it is so classified in American law. It is a stimulant acting on the central nervous system in an as yet undetermined manner.

The crumpled dried leaves and flowers of the plant (marijuana, grass, pot, tea, etc.) is the most common form of preparation of cannabis. In this form, which needs no other preparation beyond simple drying and crumbling, the drug is either smoked or brewed into a tea. It is also sometimes eaten in cookies, salads, etc. The pure resin of the plant which is carefully collected from the female flowers is commonly called hashish, kiff, or charras. This is the most potent form of the drug commonly used, being about ten times as strong as the dried leaves and flowers. Hashish is ingested by smoking or mixed into candies and pastries and eaten.

Like everything else about cannabis, there is controversy over the origin of the plant. Some botanists argue that it first grew in China and spread from there. Other experts place the site of origin in the Middle East, while still others claim this distinction for Africa. Of one thing we can be certain: Wherever it originated, cannabis has spread throughout the world. We can also be certain that wherever it grew, people discovered its medicinal and euphoric qualities. It has been estimated that upwards of 300,000,000 people throughout the world use cannabis as a drug today. Only two other drugs, alcohol and tobacco, are more widely utilized.

The history of the plant in the Western Hemisphere is equally cloudy. Most authorities believe that cannabis was introduced into the New World by European settlers. There are old records, however, cited by the writers Allen Geller and Maxwell Boas in their book *The Drug Beat* which suggest that the plant grew in the Americas before the Spanish arrivals.

Historians who accompanied the conquistadors through Mexico and South America cited cannabis preparations as elements in the religious life of the Aztec and Inca Indians. Their reports also suggest that some Spaniards were initiated into this use. The mythology of our own southwestern Indians suggests that cannabis was known among them before the arrival of Europeans.

These reports, however, are not conclusive. They may have referred to other similar hallucinogenic plants, many of which were familiar to the American Indians of both continents. We can be certain, however, that the commercial cultivation of *Cannabis sativa* was introduced to the New World very soon after European settlement. In the days of sailing ships, hemp was an indispensable commodity. The stalk of the male plant when properly processed provides long, sturdy fibers that can be woven into rope and cloth.

This cloth was used to make sails, and the rope was utilized in the complex rigging of the sailing ships. Indeed, cannabis was essential to the maritime trades, for no ship could sail without its products. Substantial crops of cannabis were growing in all the Spanish and Portuguese colonies soon after settlement to supply their ships.

When the British began to colonize the New World, they also encouraged the production of hemp. The court of King James in its patents to colonizers charged the new colonies to produce "cordage, hemp, pitch, tar and iron" for the British navy. By the early part of the seventeenth century hemp was being grown throughout New England for its fibers. Besides the maritime stores derived from the plant, cloth manufactured from the fibers became important for clothing, and during this early period most of the clothing used by the colonists was made from hemp.

In time, hemp production became centered in the Southern, more agriculturally favored states. The area around Jamestown, Virginia, became an important early center of production, but the cultivation of hemp spread throughout the plantation South and into Kentucky and Tennessee when these areas were opened to settlement. We know that George Washington and Thomas Jefferson grew hemp on their plantations. For 250 years hemp ranged behind only tobacco and later cotton as the primary cash crops of the American South.

The invention of the cotton gin in the late eighteenth century and the subsequent reduction in the cost of cotton cloth reduced the role of hemp in the manufacture of textiles, and its cultivation was subsequently limited to the production of cordage and the use of its seed in bird feed and in the extraction of oil for paints. Finally, the full blooming of the Industrial Revolution in the nineteenth century and the advent of steampower in place of sails in the maritime services put the hemp plantations out of business. Today hemp is a minor agricultural crop, whose lawful cultivation is restricted to the states of Kentucky, Illinois, Minnesota, and Wisconsin. It is grown primarily for its seed, which is an ingredient in feed for pigeons and singing birds, and for the oil which is used in the preparation of artists' paints.

Oddly enough, almost no accounts or reports have come down to us of cannabis being used as an intoxicant during the period when the plant was widely cultivated as an agricultural commodity. Although the tall, gangling plant grew almost all over America both in a wild and cultivated state, the people of that time were either unaware of the euphoric effects of the plant or did not bother to avail themselves of these controversial properties.

The one reference we do have to cannabis intoxication is oblique, but intriguing. A book titled *The Hasheesh Eater: Being Passages from the Life of a Pythagorean* was published anonymously in New York in 1860. It was purported to be a description of the harrowing experiences of the writer while under the influence of the drug. We know now that it was written by Fitzhugh Ludlow, then a schoolteacher in Poughkeepsie, New York, who had only recently been graduated from college. Ludlow apparently suffered no lasting ill effects from the drug. He survived the experience and went on to a long, successful life as a book publisher.

In writing his notorious book, young Ludlow was admittedly influenced by the writings of Thomas De Quincey of *Opium Eater* fame and by the members of the Club des Hashishins in France during this same period. His curiosity whetted by the fanciful accounts of the effects of this drug described by such writers as Charles Baudelaire and Théophile Gautier, Ludlow decided to try hashish himself. The results of his experiments are described in the book.

One of the most interesting and revealing facts in the narrative was Ludlow's account of how he went about obtaining the drug for his experiments. He went to his favorite apothecary shop in Poughkeepsie, paid the princely sum of six cents, and went home with a stick of hashish about the size of his "little finger"—a rather prosaic beginning to what Ludlow was to describe as a singular experience.

Still, the young schoolteacher's experiments with cannabis would seem to be the only account of the use of this drug in the United States prior to the twentieth century. Is it possible that even though the drug was available for nearly 300 years, no one besides Ludlow ever used it? Somehow, it does not seem likely. Hashish—the most potent form of the drug—was legally available to anyone who could pay the price of six cents for a stick. Since it was stocked in a Poughkeepsie apothecary, others besides this imaginative schoolteacher must have purchased the drug. If they did, what did they do with it?

Cannabis was, of course, used as a medicine. It was prescribed for colds, migraine headaches, and rheumatic pains and as a relaxant for sufferers of tetanus and a host of other ills. It was also widely used in veterinary medicine to quiet and relax unruly and sick animals. Surely, some of these medicinal users must have experienced the euphoric effects of the drug and come back for more.

In the pre-Civil War South, hemp was grown extensively on

plantations for its fibers, seeds, and oil. This cultivation was mainly in the hands of African field workers. We know that cannabis was used for its hallucinogenic properties all over Africa during this period. We also know that it was widely used in the West Indies by Africans and the descendants of Africans and that there was a steady migration of these unwilling immigrants between Africa, the West Indies, and the United States.

In view of this interchange, we can be certain that cannabis was smoked or ingested as a tea by black slaves in the United States in the quiet of their cabins after the long, tedious day's work was done. Phillip Ullrich in his "magnolia blossom" description of *Life and Labor in the Old South* speaks about slaves smoking the dried leaves of weeds in their pipes when they could not afford to "buy tobacco." Could the weed in question have been cannabis? Ullrich does not say, and we cannot be certain.

We can be certain, however, that the drug did not come into wide use during this period. The United States, as we have seen in Chapter 3, was an alcohol-addicted society at the time. Whiskey, gin, rum, hard cider, wine, and beer were consumed in enormous quantities on all levels of American life. The per capita consumption was staggering. And alcohol and cannabis do not generally mix. The effects of the two drugs are almost diametrically opposite.

Our forefathers were active men—they were busy conquering a continent, slaughtering Indians, kidnapping unlucky Africans to slave in their fields, amassing fortunes, fighting wars. They had little time for the smoking of a contemplative pipeful of cannabis and probably less inclination. We can be sure that George Washington never partook of the "devil weed," although he grew it on his plantation.

Thomas Jefferson, on the other hand, might have. He was, after all, of a more contemplative and philosophic disposition.

In this context it might be interesting to note a study made by Dr. George Morris Carstairs, an English psychiatrist, in India in 1951. Dr. Carstairs lived for a year in a village in the Indian state of Rajasthan in order to study the caste system that permeates Hindu society. During the course of the year, Dr. Carstairs came to know the community intimately, along with the rigid caste system which was the controlling factor in the life of the village.

An unexpected aspect of the caste system struck Dr. Carstairs as significant. He found that the people of the village revealed strong preferences according to their caste status toward the two most common intoxicants of the area—alcohol and cannabis.

The use of alcohol was limited almost exclusively to the Rajput class—the traditional warriors of India. In Rajasthan this caste held a position of social and economic dominance. They were the rulers and the large landowners. Their semifeudal authority had governed the state for centuries, and their traditional wealth and prestige were justified by their position as warriors who would fight in defense of their land and religion.

As the fighting arm of Indian society, the Rajputs had traditional privileges, notably the right to eat meat and drink alcohol. Dr. Carstairs noted that they availed themselves of these privileges generously, and a typical Rajput social affair usually became boisterous and unbridled as a result of the alcohol imbibed. Members of this caste group rarely used cannabis and looked down on those who did as impractical, slothful dreamers.

In contrast, the members of the other top caste group in the village, the Brahmins (the priestly and intellectual caste), denounced the use of alcohol. This practice, they argued, was inimical to the religious life. Religious precepts held that the first requirement for anyone who would devote himself seriously to religion was "abhorrence of meat and alcohol." Holy men insisted that those who indulged in alcohol to excess were beyond any hope of spiritual salvation. The preferred intoxicant of this priestly caste was cannabis, which they extolled as an essential aid on the path to enlightenment.

The roles played by these two distinctly different drugs in Indian society was clear. Alcohol was the intoxicant of the activists, of the rulers and doers; cannabis, of the thinkers and contemplators. Each looked down upon the choice of the other as both immoral and unseemly. Each group was adamant in its condemnation of the intoxicant of the other.

It is not difficult then to begin to understand why so little notice was taken of cannabis use in America. In the face of the staggering, belligerent, prevalent alcohol addict, who would have noticed the quiet, contemplative user of cannabis? The answer, of course, is practically no one. And so cannabis remained virtually unknown as a drug, certainly not a menace in America for nearly 300 years.

Actually, it was only in the second decade of the twentieth century that the use of cannabis attracted any official attention whatsoever in the United States. People living in the Southwest, for example, had known for generations that Mexican farm laborers who crossed the border in search of work smoked a "weed" that they called *marihuana*. There was at the time no official stigma attached to this use. Mexicans had smoked cannabis in their native land and saw no reason to alter their habits when they crossed the border into the United States.

Those Americans who were aware of the problem at all at the time looked down on cannabis as a poor man's substitute for tobacco. Certainly, it was then and remains today the least expensive of all intoxicating drugs. Before it came into conflict with the law, cannabis grew wild in practically every state in the Union. It grew abundantly in the Southwest. The Mexicans simply gathered the leaves and flowers of the wild plants, dried them, and rolled them into cigarettes. Indeed, the very name—marijuana—originally referred to the cheapest grade of tobacco used in Mexico in the manufacture of cigarettes.

In time, some of the poorer farmers and workers in the Southwest began to copy the Mexicans, and the use of cannabis spread slowly among them. Another focus for the dissemination of the drug came from the sailors who worked the ships plying between the West Indies, Central America, Mexico, and the United States. New Orleans was the major American port handling this traffic, and it is not surprising that it became the first large American city to experience a marijuana cult.

During the first two decades of the twentieth century, New Orleans became a center of cannabis use, and for a time this practice became something of a status symbol among some segments of the population. One of the reasons was the fact that jazz music was becoming increasingly popular. A new sound was coming up out of the honky-tonks and saloons of Basin Street, with a rhythm that reflected the changing tempo of American life.

A coterie of followers, fans, and devotees evolved around these early jazz musicians much as they did around rock-and-roll stars in the sixties. These fans tended to emulate their musician heroes and aped their jargon, slang, and manners.

Cannabis was an element in the jazz life, and this too was taken up by the coterie. Because of its unique ability to enhance the quality of perceived sounds, cannabis has always been closely associated with music.

It was during this period that cannabis first began to attract official attention of a negative kind. Before this time there had been no connection made between cannabis and crime. But because the first American users were predominantly members of underprivileged, which is to say disreputable groups— blacks, Mexican-Americans, Indians, sailors, laborers, and other members of the lower classes—an arbitrary connection was made between the high crime rates in these groups and their use of cannabis. That these groups have a higher crime rate and a higher incidence of the more violent felonies whether they smoked cannabis or not was not considered. The fact that these problems derived more from the economic and social status of the people involved than from their use of cannabis was ignored.

Actually, there were a number of official, scientific investigations made into the use of cannabis. The most ambitious, the *British East India Hemp Commission Report*, prepared in 1893–94 and published in 1894, ran to seven volumes and more than 3,000 pages. With typical English objectivity and thoroughness, the commission studied all phases of cannabis use in a country where the drug had been in common use for centuries. They interviewed hundreds of users and made detailed observations on the effects of the drug on both the individuals involved and the society as a whole.

Their findings were anything but sensational. They reported that cannabis was not an addictive drug in the sense that opium and alcohol are; they could detect no significant physical effects or evidence of mental deterioration in moderate users and found no causal connection with crime of any kind. Cannabis, the report concluded, was a mild intoxicant sanctioned by a society that had used the drug for thousands of years. The commission recommended that the colonial government not interfere with the traffic of the drug as it was then organized in India.

A study made by the U.S. Army into the growing use of cannabis among soldiers stationed in Panama revealed similar findings:

> After an investigation extending from April to December 1925, the committee reached the following conclusions: There is no evidence that marijuana as grown here is a "habit-forming" drug in the sense to which the term is applied to alcohol, opium, cocaine, etc., or that it has any appreciable deleterious influence upon the individual using it.

These studies were ignored, and a concentrated effort to link cannabis and crime was instituted. Thus began one of the strangest, most grotesque chapters in American legal history. A hoax of monstrous proportion was perpetrated on the American people—a hoax, for it can be called nothing less, that has done incalculable damage over the years and whose effects continue to take a toll to this day.

It began with a number of sensational articles that appeared in New Orleans newspapers during the early 1920's. In one of them, Dr. R. Gomila, commissioner of public safety in New Orleans, wrote that homes for wayward boys were "full of children who had become habituated to the use of cannabis." He went on to describe "marihuana-crazed" youngsters who slaughtered policemen, bank clerks, and casual bystanders in a mad frenzy induced by the drug. Dr. Gomila attributed 68 percent of the crime committed in New Orleans at the time to the "killer-drug." An odd statement, if only because the figure is so precise—68 percent; why not 70 percent or 65 percent?

At first these reports attracted little attention despite their lurid and sensational nature. America, at the time, was in the midst of Prohibition, and alcohol consumption and illegal bootlegging were the major topics of interest to the moralists. But then two factors came onto the scene which turned things around. Prohibition was repealed—alcohol was no longer an official menace and crime—and in 1930 the Federal Narcotics Bureau was instituted as a part of the Treasury Department. Its first director was Harry J. Anslinger. Repeal of Prohibition left a huge gap in the reformer's zeal—a vacuum, as it were, that had to be filled. The establishment of the Narcotics Bureau created an organization that had to find justification for its existence. Both needs could be satisfied by cannabis.

There was only one problem: Very few people in America had heard about cannabis. The use of the drug was restricted to a tiny portion of the population, and it is difficult to get people excited about something they know nothing about. Mr. Anslinger, the new chief of the Narcotics Bureau, was aware of the problem and took steps to remedy the situation. In a book titled *The Murderers*, which was co-authored by Fulton Oursler, Mr. Anslinger described his efforts to arouse an apathetic public:

> As the marijuana situation grew worse, I knew action had to be taken to get proper legislation passed. . . . Much of the irrational juvenile violence and killing that has written a new chapter of shame and tragedy is traceable directly to hemp intoxication. . . . On radio and at major forums . . . I told

the story of this evil weed of the fields and rivers and roadsides. I wrote articles for magazines; our agents gave hundreds of lectures to parents, educators, social and civic leaders. In network broadcasts I reported on the growing list of crimes including murder and rape. I described the nature of marijuana. . . . I continued to hammer at the facts. . . . I believe we did a thorough job, for the public was alerted, and the laws to protect them were passed, both nationally and at the state level.

Typical of this "civic-minded" education was a pamphlet titled *Marihuana or Indian Hemp and Its Preparations* issued in 1936 by the International Narcotic Education Association. It was prepared in cooperation with the Narcotics Bureau and received wide circulation:

Prolonged use of marihuana frequently develops a delirious rage which sometimes leads to high crimes such as assault and murder. Hence marihuana has been called the "killer drug." The habitual use of this narcotic poison always causes a very marked mental deterioration and sometimes produces insanity. Hence marihuana is frequently called "loco weed."

While the marihuana habit leads to physical wreckage and mental decay, its effects upon the character and morality are even more devastating. The victim frequently undergoes such degeneracy that he will lie and steal without scruple; he becomes utterly untrustworthy and often drifts into the underworld where, with his degenerate companions, he commits high crimes and misdemeanors. Marihuana often gives man the lust to kill unreasonably and without motive. Many cases of assault, rape, robbery and murder are traced to the use of marihuana.

As was to be expected, cannabis attracted the attention of the reformers and moralists. Typical of these was Albert Rowell, who had also zealously combated the evils of alcohol and tobacco. Mr. Rowell boasted that he had spent fourteen years campaigning against this "killer weed" during which time he gave more than 4,000 lectures in forty states, in all of which he spent his free time tearing up fields of wild hemp. The heart of his stand against the cannabis menace were summed up in a poster that listed eight points and which was widely circulated:

We know that marihuana—
1. Destroys will power, making a jellyfish of the user. He cannot say no!
2. Eliminates the line between right and wrong, and substitutes one's own warped desires or the base suggestions of others as the standard of right.
3. Above all, causes crime; fills the victim with an irrepressible urge to violence.
4. Incites to revolting immoralities, including rape and murder.
5. Causes many accidents both industrial and automobile.
6. Ruins careers forever.
7. Causes insanity as its specialty.
8. Either in self-defense or as a means of revenue, users make smokers of others, thus perpetuating evil.

As though on cue, the popular press followed suit. A rash of sensational scare stories appeared in newspapers and magazines across the country. Most of these were either prepared by or influenced by the Narcotics Bureau publicity campaign. Then the book publishers joined the chorus. Some titles from the period reveal the lurid aspects of this material: *Sex Crazing*

Drug Menace; *Marihuana as a Developer of Criminals*; *Exposing the Marihuana Drug Evil in Swing Bands*; etc. In the Depression days of the mid-1930's, when the nation was racked by economic crises, this kind of fare proved popular among readers. Perhaps it took people's minds off their real economic troubles.

There was only one thing wrong with the campaign: The great bulk of this alarmist literature had no basis in fact. There was little attempt to document the lurid stories; there was no scientific evaluation of the reported mental and physical damage attributed to the drug; and almost no effort was made to separate fact from fancy. Indeed, most of the stories were made up—composed in the city rooms of the nation's newspapers by feature writers hoping to boost sales. In short, a menace was created through the concentrated efforts of the Narcotics Bureau and the enthusiastic cooperation of the mass media.

By the spring of 1937, when the Marihuana Tax Bill was enacted by Congress, most people in America had heard about the drug. Many of them believed, sincerely, that abuse of the drug was growing in epidemic proportions and that the nation was on the verge of being engulfed in a wave of crime, mayhem, and moral degeneracy as a result of the use of cannabis.

Harry J. Anslinger was right. The Narcotics Bureau had done a thorough job. The nation was alerted. How thorough this "educational" program had been can be seen by comparing two reports made by the Narcotics Bureau itself. In 1932 the bureau's annual report for the preceding year stated that:

A great deal of public interest has been aroused by newspaper articles appearing from time to time on the evils of the abuse of marihuana, or Indian hemp, and more attention has been focused on specific cases reported of the abuse of the drug than the incidents themselves warrant. This publicity tends to magnify the extent of the evil and lends color to the inference that there is an alarming spread of the improper use of the drug whereas the actual increase in such use may not have been inordinately large.

Five years later, in a hearing before the Ways and Means Committee, which was considering passage of antimarijuana legislation, Mr. Anslinger's testimony had changed dramatically. He presented marijuana as a menace of crisis proportion that was spreading like a cancer through the nation. If allowed to remain unchecked, Mr. Anslinger implied, this abuse could spell the doom of society. When asked why this legislation had not been proposed sooner in the light of the dire danger of the drug, Mr. Anslinger explained: "Ten years ago we only heard about it throughout the southwest. It is only in the last few years that it has become a national menace."

Needless to say, the Marihuana Tax Bill was passed almost unanimously by both houses of Congress. Objections raised by commercial hemp-seed oil producers and bird feed companies were quickly met, and the bill became law. There were no representatives of users of the drug at the hearings, and there was no attempt made to check the validity of the sensational reports. A law was passed which arbitrarily made criminals out of the users of a drug that Colonel J. M. Phalen, editor of the *Military Surgeon*, described after an official inquiry as "no more harmful than the smoking of tobacco or mullein or sumac leaves. . . . The legislation in relation to marihuana was ill-advised . . . it branded as a menace and a crime a matter of trivial importance."

In response to the same tactics, state after state passed

antimarijuana legislation along with the federal law. Some states, in their enthusiasm to combat the menace, passed laws that were far harsher than the federal legislation. The state of Georgia, for example, made the sale of marijuana to a minor a capital offense punishable by death.

In that period of ramrod legislation only Mayor Fiorello LaGuardia of New York City appealed to reason. As a Congressman he had studied the U.S. Army commission report on marijuana use by soldiers stationed in Panama in 1925. This commission, you will recall, after a six-month study into the drug failed to detect any dire dangers in the use of the drug by Army personnel. In order realistically to evaluate the situation in New York City, Mayor LaGuardia appointed a committee of doctors and psychologists to make a detailed, objective study of marijuana and its effects on users and its relationship to the criminal life of the city.

This report was finally published in 1944 after a great deal of objection by the Narcotics Bureau and federal law enforcement agencies. The committee report, it turned out, was very similar in its findings to the earlier study of cannabis use made by a British team in India. To the consternation of the "menace peddlers" the LaGuardia committee found that marijuana was a mild euphoriant that was not addictive, had negligible physiological effects on the user, was not an element in crime, and did not lead to physical, mental, or moral degeneration and that no permanent deleterious effects from its continued use were observed.

The committee also reported that marijuana use was not widespread and was confined mainly to black ghetto areas and to a small bohemian fringe of musicians, writers, and artists. They found no evidence of the reported epidemic spread of the use and saw no reason to consider the drug a menace.

The report was attacked by those committed to a belief in the marijuana scare. Harry J. Anslinger, for example, criticized the findings of the committee in a series of letters published in the *Journal of the American Medical Association* and was supported in his views by the editorial policy of this journal. Officially, of course, the report was ignored. It was too little and too late. The antimarijuana laws remained in effect, and the sensational scare stories continued to be circulated.

The Narcotics Bureau had created a dragon and then with the aid of the antimarijuana laws proceeded to slay it. There was a flurry of arrests in the late 1930's after the laws had gone into effect; several cities instituted campaigns to wipe out the "menace." Since there was no menace to begin with, the efforts of the Narcotics Bureau and law enforcement agencies enlisted in this battle were eminently successful. The danger had been averted. They could point to the fact that hospitals and asylums were not being overrun with marijuana-induced psychotics; that streets were safe from drug-frenzied killers running amok; that the epidemic growth in the use of marijuana had been checked as fruits of their efforts.

And indeed, the menace appeared to have all but disappeared. After the initial flurry of enforcement in the late thirties, the number of marijuana arrests steadily declined. By 1960 it was close to the vanishing point with only some 169 cases reported for the year throughout the nation.

Then, in the early 1960's, something happened. In what may well be the most exciting decade in American history, the nation experienced what can only be described as a change in consciousness. This change was revealed, in part, in an eruption of creativity that literally dazzled the world. A new, exciting music swept the scene, bubbling up out of America's black ghettos and churches to engulf America and the world in a torrent of liberating, sensuous sound. American artists working in Manhattan lofts and Chicago studios, storefronts in San Francisco, and barns in Minnesota discovered a new way of looking at the world that gave rise to a host of new schools and styles whose vigor and inventiveness penetrated the very foundations of the visual arts. Poetry was reborn as a vital, living literary form that spoke in concrete syntax of the terror and joy of this new consciousness.

This creative eruption was revealed in a new life-style that appeared to threaten the structure of established order. Hair sprouted ominously all over America. The crew-cut, clean-shaved military look disappeared under shoulder-length hair and chest-long beards. The gray flannel suit gave way to dungarees and loose, open-necked shirts. The tie was replaced by a string of beads. Communes sprouted like mushrooms from the slums of New York's Lower East Side to the deserts of Arizona and New Mexico. A strange children's crusade came into being with hordes of youngsters leaving hearth and home to roam the land, attracted like iron filings to the magnets of the Haight-Ashbury and St. Marks Place. Everyone, it seemed, was ready to try something new—to burst out of old traditions and ruts.

One of the new things turned out to be that old bugaboo—cannabis. As though confirming the worst nightmare of the Narcotics Bureau, the use of marijuana spread like a contagion to all levels of American society. It spread from the bohemian fringes and the black ghettos to the colleges, from the colleges to the professional world, from the private jam sessions to the public music festivals, from the hippie communes to high society. Everyone, it seemed, was ready to try this new kick. Today estimates of the number of people who have used marijuana range as high as 35,000,000, and the number continues to grow.

Why this sudden popularity of an experience that had for so long been confined to only a limited stratum of society?

The answer will probably never be fully understood, but we can cite several factors that bear on the question. One, of course, is that change of consciousness which has shaken all of American society. America and the world have passed into a new phase. The threat of atomic destruction looms over us like an obscuring cloud. There are no more heroes, and even our history has been stripped of pretense. In this new world our Founding Fathers are seen as slaveowners mouthing pious words about freedom and democracy as masks for the maintenance of their own privileges. The conquest of the West, once such a glorious chapter in our history, is seen today as the cruel, genocidal attrition of the original Indian inhabitants. The spectacular growth of American industry is seen as the rape of the natural world in which its beauty and wealth have been greedily despoiled.

It is a phase in which there has been a subtle turning within, in which people are beginning to explore themselves—their inner lives and inner experiences. This change has been revealed in the spread of contemplative religions, in the growth of the encounter experience. And it is this factor, probably more than anything else, that is responsible for the spectacular rise in marijuana use. This is the traditional drug of the contemplator, the drug that has been most strongly identified with the religious experience.

Another element in this spread is the fact that for the first time in American history influential people have openly advocated the use of marijuana and have extolled some of its beneficial properties. The novelist William Burroughs, for example, sees marijuana as: "unquestionably very useful to the artist, activating trains of association that would otherwise be inaccessible . . . cannabis serves as a guide to psychic areas which can then be re-entered without it . . . it would seem that cannabis . . . provides a key to the creative process."

The poet Allen Ginsberg claims that the drug "ever so gently shifts the center of attention from habitual shallow purely verbal guidelines and repetitive secondhand ideological interpretation of experience to more direct, slower, absorbing, occasionally microscopically minute engagement with sensing phenomena during the high moments or hours after one has smoked."

Finally, there is the element of youth revolt that cannot be discounted. Youth and age have always been in conflict, but this particular generation appears to have deliberately intensified the gap. They have taken George Bernard Shaw's adage to heart: "Look to your elders as a warning, not as an example." Parents do not smoke "pot"; *ergo*, "WE WILL!"

Although the lurid dangers of cannabis tend to shrink or dissolve entirely when subjected to close, impartial examination, antimarijuana laws still exist. People are still being arrested and subjected to all the harassment that the Establishment can enlist. A virtual army of law officers, undercover agents, and informers—with all their unsavory tactics—continue to operate against the "menace."

Of course, the arguments have changed somewhat. In the thirties it was claimed that cannabis use leads to insanity, rape, murder, and other miscellaneous mayhems. Today this aspect is played down. The menace now is the belief that marijuana use leads inevitably to the living hell of heroin addiction. This belief, like the old bugaboos, also appears to have very little basis in fact. Statistical evidence fails to bear out this interesting assumption.

Although practically every commission that has studied the drug—including a Presidential commission that reported in the spring of 1972—has recommended changes in the harsh laws, those changes have not been forthcoming. Why? Perhaps the menace has been oversold; perhaps Congress is reluctant to admit that it made a serious mistake in passing the laws in the first place; perhaps it is just a natural reluctance to change the status quo. Whatever the reasons, the use of cannabis remains a crime in the United States, and it does not appear likely that this situation will change in the near future.

The poet Allen Ginsberg explains this apparent paradox this way:

> When the citizens of this country see that such an old-time, taken-for-granted, flag-waving, reactionary truism of police, press, and law as the "reefer menace" is in fact a creepy hoax, a scarecrow, a national hallucination emanating from the perverted brain of one single man (perhaps) such as Anslinger, what will they begin to think of the whole taken-for-granted public REALITY? What of the other issues filled with the same threatening hysteria? The spectre of Communism? Respect for the police and courts? Respect for the Treasury Department? If marihuana is a hoax, what is Money? What is the war in Viet Nam? What are the Mass Media?

6. THE WHITE PLAGUE

THE opium poppy (*Papaver somniferum*) is a lovely plant. When well grown, most varieties are tall, reaching a height of three to four feet. The flowers are large and showy, measuring some four to five inches across, and may be white, pink, red, purple, or lavender. The most common cultivated variety is white with a spot of violet or red at the base of the petals. Such a field in full bloom is an impressive sight, "like a field of rippling snow," according to one observer.

Foliage of the poppy is smooth to the touch and of a peculiar whitish green color. Most plants consist of a main stem that ends in the largest flower and seed capsule with side branches that end in smaller flowers and capsules. Even the tiniest seedling can be readily identified chemically because of the presence of morphine in the sap.

Papaver somniferum is a hardy plant that grows readily in practically any soil throughout the temperate zone. It does, however, prefer a rather dry climate especially in the fall at the time of harvest. Seeds are generally sown in late autumn, and the crop is harvested the following summer. The plant can also be seeded in early spring, but in this case the harvest will be several weeks later than the autumn sown crop.

As an agricultural commodity the plant is grown for its seeds, which are considered a delicacy and are eaten almost all over the world (the seed is the only part of the plant which does not contain opiates); for its leaves, which are eaten in salads; as a decorative plant for the handsome flowers and seed capsules which are dried and glossed; as a feed for cattle and other livestock; and for the juice of the plant which provides a veritable cornucopia of drugs.

The opium poppy is nature's great synthesizer of drugs, producing some fifty distinctive substances that have pronounced effects on the human body and psyche. Out of air, water, soil, and sunshine the prolific poppy creates opium, morphine, noscapine, papaverine, cotarnine, narceine, ethylmorphine, nalorphine, codeine, hydromorphone, metopone, apomorphine, dihydromorphine, thebaine, hydrocodone, hydrocodeine, etc., etc., etc., and, of course, heroin.

This mother lode of narcotic drugs is harvested by carefully cutting thin, shallow slits into the seedpod just before the petals are about to fall and collecting the sap that oozes out of the incisions. This is generally done once during the growing season; but in some areas two incisions are made, and the sap is collected twice. In this case, however, there is generally a smaller percentage of morphine in the sap collected from the second incision. Harvesting requires a great deal of painstaking hand labor since incision and collecting cannot be done by machine.

Modern agricultural methods, however, are being applied to the opium harvest in some parts of the world, mechanizing what has always been an arduous task of hand labor. A technique developed in Hungary, as one example, utilizes harvesting machinery to reap the mature poppy plants. The plants—stalk, leaves, capsule and all—are then crushed to extract the sap. Drug yields in this method, however, are somewhat less per plant than those achieved in hand collection.

The opium poppy is believed to have originated in the eastern Mediterranean area, in what is now Israel, Lebanon, Turkey, Greece, Yugoslavia, and possibly Italy. It was probably first domesticated for its seed, though knowledge of its narcotic qualities appears to be extremely old. We know that it was cultivated in Neolithic villages throughout the eastern Mediterranean region at least 15,000 years ago. From there culture of the plant spread through central and eastern Europe well before the historical epoch began.

Opium as a drug was already known in ancient Mesopotamia some 5,000 years ago. The plant, methods for extracting opium, which was called lion's fat, and the medicinal properties of the drug all were described in medical texts written on cuneiform tablets. The Egyptians grew the plant and used opium both medicinally and recreationally. Homer described the poppy plant in the *Odyssey*, where it was brewed into a tea and offered as a beverage of hospitality to travelers. Dioscorides, a Greek physician of the first century A.D., described the medicinal properties of modern opium with scientific precision.

From these lands the culture of the opium poppy spread eastward in a slow migration. Apparently, it was unknown in India and China before about A.D. 1000. The widespread cultivation of *Papaver somniferum* in these areas is a comparatively recent development. Although some knowledge of opium may have reached India and China somewhat earlier, cultivation did not begin until this period. Opium reached

Japan in the fifteenth century when cultivation of the poppy for the drug was first begun.

Opium smoking—the traditional vice of the Far East—did not, in any case, begin until well after the discovery of America. There was no custom of smoking anything in Europe, Asia, or Africa. This practice was developed in North and South America and was introduced to the rest of the world after the discoveries of Columbus and other European explorers.

Actually, the smoking of opium first became a problem in China and India only in the late eighteenth and early nineteenth centuries and then mainly as a result of enterprising British and American merchants. Traders from both countries had discovered that opium was an ideal commodity on which vast sums could be made. It was inexpensive and easy to transport and, best of all, could be sold at substantial profit.

Trade in opium soon became indispensable to the vast financial empire of the British East India Company. Revenues from sale of the drugs, which British merchants introduced into China, helped finance the administration of Britain's Far Eastern colonies, while the profits which accrued to the East India Company were central to the industrial development of Great Britain. The trade also became the cause of a war between Britain and China in 1839–42—the infamous Opium War.

What happened was the Chinese government sought to prevent the import of opium into China. These imports had grown so large, so quickly, that their cost strained an already-shaky Chinese fiscal system. The continued outflow of silver and gold to pay for the drug put an intolerable pressure on the Chinese economy. Although it was admittedly a secondary consideration, Chinese officials also looked askance at the growing dependency on opium shown by so many of its nationals. England, of course, refused to tolerate this barbaric restraint of "international trade."

In the time-honored European tradition of settling mercantile disputes, England went to war. It began when a Chinese commissioner, at the order of the Chinese imperial court, seized and destroyed a warehouseful of British and American opium in Canton. The British government—defender of civilization and commerce—acted swiftly.

The war, of course, was completely one-sided. When it ended, the Chinese government had to pay indemnities not only for the opium destroyed in Canton, but also for the loss to British interests in the opium trade during hostilities, plus the cost to the British government for waging the war. The peace treaty that ended hostilities also called for an "open door" policy which allowed European and American merchants access to all Chinese ports while allowing them extraterritorial privileges in these areas.

British interests, of course, enjoyed the lion's share of the lucrative opium traffic in China, but American interests also had a finger in this profitable pie. By 1839, on the eve of the Opium War, one American firm, Russell and Company of Boston, ranked as the third largest importer of opium into China. So extensive was American involvement in the trade that the Chinese mayor at Canton believed that Turkey was a colony of the United States because so much Turkish opium was exported to China in American ships.

Many of the great New England family fortunes were based on the shipping industry in which opium trade with China played a major role. A century later the fortune of one such family, the Delanos, helped lift Franklin Delano Roosevelt to the Presidency of the United States. Indeed, money earned in the opium trade helped finance the railroads that opened the West and provided cheap labor—also from China—to help construct the railroads.

Here, again, we have a drug figuring prominently in the economic development of America. Alcohol, tobacco, and also opium played significant roles in this history. Actually, this should not be surprising. From the seller's point of view, drugs are the ideal commodity. Once a market is established, it renews and perpetuates itself without further effort, and the seller can charge whatever the traffic will bear with no consideration for what the product may actually cost. There are very few other areas where so much money can be made so quickly.

Today's market in illegal heroin provides a perfect case in point. According to government estimates, some $25 worth of opium when processed into heroin and sold on the streets will bring in about $200,000—a handsome profit margin indeed, even considering exaggeration of the figures!

Ah well, who knows what future American Presidents will be financed by fortunes made in today's illicit traffic in heroin?

In the Western Hemisphere opium was unknown before the advent of Europeans. And even Europeans at the time knew opium primarily as a medicine, not as a recreational drug. It was as a medicine that opium first came into the New World. The Pilgrims undoubtedly brought it along on the *Mayflower* in the form of laudanum—a tincture containing about 10 percent opium by volume—and paregoric—a mixture of opium, camphor, and alcohol.

Laudanum was first compounded by Paracelsus, the Swiss physician and alchemist (1493–1541), who extolled its medicinal virtues. In a letter (*circa* 1530) Paracelsus wrote: "I possess a secret remedy which I call laudanum and which is superior to all other remedies." The Swiss physician prescribed laudanum for a wide variety of ills and it became a popular medicine throughout Europe. It was used in the treatment of almost every disease known and was part of the pharmacopoeia of every physician.

Vials of laudanum were undoubtedly brought to the New World with the first European settlers. The medicine was sipped as a general tonic and as a cure for coughs, rheumatism, stomach upset, diarrhea, arthritis, and practically any other ill that may have befallen a colonist. Throughout the seventeenth and eighteenth centuries, laudanum was an important element in the trade in medicinal drugs between England and its colonies.

Although laudanum, paregoric, and other opium-based medicines were used widely during the colonial period, we have no evidence that the drug was ever "abused" in any marked degree. Again, as in the case of marijuana, those who used opium recreationally—not primarily as a medicine— may not have been noticed. Alcohol was consumed in such great quantity by so many during this period that it eclipsed all other drug abuse. As a medicine, however, we know that opiates in a number of forms were widely prescribed by doctors.

One such physician, Dr. Benjamin Rush—a signer of the Declaration of Independence—was typical. He prescribed opium freely and recommended it as a cure for coughs, stomach upsets, malaria, tuberculosis, rheumatism, and such children's ailments as teething problems, whooping cough, and *restlessness*. One of the nation's early prohibitionists, Dr. Rush was one of the first physicians to look upon alcoholism as a disease rather than a symptom of moral weakness.

In very contemporary-sounding terms, he argued for medical treatment for alcoholics and sought the cause of the disease in a biological affinity for alcohol in some people. One of the treatments Dr. Rush recommended was the gradual replacement of alcohol by opium. His contention, based on sound medical logic, was that since opium was so much less toxic than alcohol, it was better for the patient to be habituated to the less dangerous drug!

It must be remembered that medical practice at the time was rather primitive, and Dr. Rush's recommendations must be considered in the context of the day. Though forward-looking in some respects, many of the remedies he advocated would be frowned on by today's doctors. For example, part of Dr. Rush's treatment of tuberculosis consisted in having patients chop wood while heavily bundled up in order to work up a good sweat, ride horseback, and hike vigorously through the woods.

He also had singular remedies for the prevalent malaria and yellow fever that plagued so many colonists. In his papers, Dr. Rush appears to have been especially proud of his success in treating one victim of yellow fever. This patient, obviously a man of robust constitution, survived a regimen that included the loss of a gallon of blood in six days through medicinal bloodletting, ingesting 150 grains of calomel (a powerful purgative and a slow poison that is no longer ingested as a medicine), and remaining in a room without windows or vents for the length of treatment. In his journals, Dr. Rush neglects to mention the patients who succumbed to this heroic treatment who might otherwise have survived.

Throughout the first half of the nineteenth century, opium was regularly prescribed in the treatment of ailments suffered by children, as well as adults, but it never did become a problem. There is no mention of addiction as we know it today in the medical records of the period, in the law records, or even in the preachings of the moralists. Opium was looked upon and accepted as a medicine. If some patients tended to take too much, it was considered no more than zeal in looking after one's health.

Then, in the mid-nineteenth century, two developments changed this attitude completely. One was the entrance into the Western states of large numbers of Chinese workmen, who were brought into the country as a source of cheap labor for the construction of railroads. The second pivotal event was the Civil War.

Now the Chinese workmen imported to build the railroads did not leave their customs behind when they came to America. They brought them with them. One of these customs, thanks to the vigorous enterprise of English and American merchants, was the smoking of opium. The people took the drug as a recreational activity. They smoked for *pleasure*—not for treatment or alleviation of any medical condition or complaint. Their use of opium was similar in most respects to the social drinking of alcoholic beverages among Americans and Europeans.

With the arrival of the Chinese and their custom of smoking opium as a recreational drug, we get our first reports of a "problem." Opium dens, where Chinese came to smoke opium pipes, appeared in San Francisco, Los Angeles, and other Western cities and towns that had sizable Chinese populations. These dens were habituated only by Chinese at first, but then they were discovered. The first to take notice were the authorities—the police, followed quickly by newspaper reporters and moralists. All spread sensational stories about the horrors and immoralities of these "pits of Oriental depravity."

Appropriate laws were swiftly passed to protect the public. The first such anti-opium law was passed in San Francisco in 1875, Virginia City, Nevada, enacted a similar ordinance in 1876, and other Western cities and towns followed soon after.

Then, as has happened before and since so many times, the sensational stories and repressive laws attracted an army of eager voluptuaries anxious to experience a new thrill. For many, the promise of "Oriental depravity" was an enticement that could not be resisted. White people began to patronize Chinese opium dens in larger numbers despite the laws and threat of punishment. Indeed, it appeared as though the repressive laws and scare stories stimulated the interest in opium smoking among people who had never even heard of the vice before.

The practice of smoking opium in "dens" spread rapidly throughout the country. By the end of the nineteenth century such establishments could be found in every city. An exposé in *Harper's Magazine* in 1882 described luxurious smoking dens habituated by wealthy sensualists and criminal elements in New York, Boston and Philadelphia. In the mid-nineteenth century, also, we get our first reports of opium being used nonmedically in bohemian and intellectual circles. This use was probably stimulated by the writings of Thomas De Quincey—the "Opium Eater"—and by the writings of the members of the Club des Hashishins in France. In America, it was reported that Edgar Allan Poe, among other writers and artists, was an "opium-eater."

At this time, however, there was no concept of addiction in the sense we know it today. The term was not even applied to alcoholism. Although some doctors recognized the compulsive character of alcohol addiction and understood physical tolerance and withdrawal symptoms, this recognition was not widespread. The chronic drunkard was looked on as a person of moral weakness rather than one in need of medical and psychological help.

Opium addiction was unknown. It was recognized as neither a medical nor a social problem. Certainly, physicians of the time were aware that many patients appeared to have an inordinate craving for opium-based drugs, but this was not looked on as deviant behavior. During this period, it must be remembered, opium was available to anyone who wanted to buy it in a variety of forms and preparations at all pharmacies. Marijuana, hashish, cocaine, and other drugs were also available legally with no governmental proscription. As we look back at the period today, it would seem to have been a drug addict's paradise.

The next big milestone in the history of narcotics came with the isolation of morphine as the principal analgesic alkaloid of opium. This interesting substance was first isolated by Friedrich W. A. Sertürner, a German chemist, in 1806. This natural alkaloid of opium makes up about 10 to 15 percent of opium extracted from the poppy plant. Noting the marked analgesic qualities of the substance, Sertürner named the alkaloid after Morpheus, Greek god of dreams.

In isolating morphine, Sertürner discovered one of the most important drugs in the medical pharmacopoeia. It is still indispensable in the treatment and relief of pain of all kinds. Indeed, most physicians would agree that it would be all but impossible to treat patients in many, many cases without morphine.

In many respects, morphine is the ideal analgesic. It stops pain; it is not toxic even after extended use; it has few side effects; it is easy to administer; and it is inexpensive. The one drawback, of course, is the fact that morphine is highly addictive. Once physical tolerance is effected, the user must have his or her daily dose of morphine in order to function normally. It is this need, rather than any euphoria, or high, that is at the basis of addiction. The addict is compelled to take the drug in order to feel "normal," not for any desire for euphoria or ecstasy.

As an analgesic, morphine appears to act directly on the central nervous system. Actually, however, we do not know how it works. Most authorities agree that the drug seems to depress a pain center in the cortex. This depressive effect is highly selective. It appears to alter the perception of pain without affecting the sense of touch, taste, hearing, smell, or sight.

Psychologically, its action is peculiar. Morphine raises the tolerable level of pain. The patient, under influence of the drug, can withstand pain that would be unbearable without the drug. Most significantly, morphine relieves the anxiety and fear associated with pain so that while the pain is known to be present, it can be regarded with equanimity and detachment as though it were occurring to someone else.

In the generally administered dosage, morphine does not induce sleep, though more massive doses will. One of the problems with morphine is that an overdose can cause a trancelike state than can lead to fatal respiratory failure. This, of course, is the chief hazard in the use of both morphine and heroin. Death by overdose, however, is comparatively rare despite the sensational publicity given to drug deaths which are almost always listed as OD's (overdose). Most deaths attributed to OD are, in fact, the results of a complex syndrome that is not well understood, but may involve adulterants in black-market heroin in combination with alcohol.

The usual medical dosage in mild to moderate pain is 5 to 10 milligrams taken orally, which generally produces an analgesic effect that lasts four to five hours without sedation (that is, the patient will remain awake), about one to one and a half hours after being taken. When injected intravenously, morphine reaches its peak effect within minutes, but the analgesic action is shorter in duration, lasting no more than two to three hours in most cases.

The most commonly used method for administering morphine is by subcutaneous injection (skin popping, in the vernacular), in which analgesia occurs within twenty to thirty minutes and lasts almost as long as an oral dose. The principal drawback to oral administration is the fact that it takes so long for analgesia to occur and a much larger dosage is required for the same analgesic effect. Eight milligrams injected have about the same effect as 60 milligrams taken orally.

Morphine did not come into general medical use until some forty years after its discovery. It had to wait for one other important medical development—the hypodermic syringe, introduced in 1853, which allowed administration of medication directly into the bloodstream. Actually, it was not until the Civil War in the United States (1861–1865) that morphine was used extensively as a medical analgesic. In many respects, this conflict was the first truly "modern" war in history. It consumed men and materials on a scale that dwarfed all earlier conflicts, and in its involvement of the civilian population it anticipated the terrible destruction of later wars.

It also marked the first extensive use of hypodermically injected morphine to relieve pain. Morphine was administered to hundreds of thousands of soldiers who were wounded in battle. It was also administered generously and freely with a resulting wave of addicted patients.

Indeed, morphine addiction became so common during and immediately following the Civil War that it came to be known as soldiers' disease. For the first time in medical history, doctors recognized addiction as a medical problem. They realized that the craving for morphine exhibited by addicted patients was so strong that the victim could not function normally without having this need satisfied.

With the recognition of addiction as a medical condition came the realization that many more people besides soldiers were afflicted. It must be remembered, however, that this recognition came slowly. It took many years, for example, to realize that addiction to morphine injected hypodermically was the same as addiction to an opium-based patent medicine. Narcotics addiction was obviously a subtle condition that was not immediately recognizable.

The difficulty in medically identifying addiction is further demonstrated by the history of heroin. Heroin was developed in 1898 by the Bayer Company in Germany as a more potent analgesic than morphine. It was also discovered that heroin relieved morphine-withdrawal symptoms, which was then a perplexing medical problem, and was hailed as a cure for addiction to morphine. Heroin was used in this fashion by doctors all over the world for some fifteen years before it was discovered that heroin, too, was addicting!

By the year 1890 it was estimated that there were as many as 1,000,000 people in America—more than half of them women—who were addicted to the opiates in patent medicines; another 200,000 to 300,000—a large percentage veterans of the Civil War—addicted to morphine; at least 100,000 regular smokers of opium; and a growing bohemian fringe of artists and writers who were emulating fashionable European "opium eaters."

Statistics compiled by the customs officials on the amounts of opiates imported into the United States following the Civil War offer a graphic picture of the increase in narcotic use during this period:

1860–1869	110,305 pounds
1870–1879	195,995 "
1880–1889	352,685 "
1890–1899	513,850 "

During the first two decades of the twentieth century the figure had climbed to more than 100,000 pounds annually!

These were the "good old days"—a time we look back on today with nostalgia as a period of innocence and benevolence. How did a society with a total population of about 90,000,000 handle some 1,500,000 addicts? The answer, of course, was they handled them adroitly. Despite the addict population, America prospered, grew, and developed in every aspect. Most addicts of the time, however, did not know they were addicted. They just knew that their favorite tonic or elixir made them feel better and that they felt terrible without their daily dose!

This state of affairs might have continued indefinitely except for international developments. As we have already seen, traffic in opium was a mainstay of England's Far Eastern trade. British merchants dominated this trade, though American interests were also involved on a small scale. Traffic in opium, like all other trade, centered on China with its vast population and market potential.

Then, after the Spanish-American War, the United States emerged as an imperial power with interests of its own in the Orient. "Manifest Destiny" had somehow become extended from California clear across the Pacific Ocean to China and Japan—England, of course, had India all sewn up and French interests were entrenched in Indochina, while the Dutch were in the East Indies.

Britain had been criticized for shipping opium into China for many years. Now Americans joined the chorus. American missionaries in China complained that English opium was leading the people into sin and degeneracy, that it was ruining the Chinese people. More significantly, however, American traders complained that the silver being spent for English drugs could better be used for useful American manufactured products. The agitation against British opium sales to China continued until finally, at the request of the Right Reverend Charles H. Brent, Episcopal Bishop of the Philippine Islands, an international conference was called by President Theodore Roosevelt. Two meetings were held, one in Shanghai in 1909 and the other in The Hague in 1911–12.

The Hague Conference, in effect, sought to regulate international traffic in opium. More important, however, the language of the agreement identified opium addiction as a high moral crime. Opium smoking became something more than just an expensive, highly compulsive habit—it became a sign of moral degeneracy. British merchants in the trade who objected on grounds that smoking opium was no more heinous or damaging than smoking tobacco and certainly much safer than drinking gin were overruled in the atmosphere of righteous indignation that pervaded the conference.

Meanwhile, back in America, the great moral problem racking the nation was Prohibition. There were no antiopiate forces of appreciable strength and organization. There were sensational stories circulated about colorful "opium dens," and doctors were aware that addiction to morphine was growing and was difficult to treat; but there was no concentrated outcry against opiates and narcotics as such.

Passage of the Harrison Act in 1914 was accomplished, mainly to fulfill our obligations under the Hague Treaty of 1912. The principal proponent of the measure was William Jennings Bryan, the Secretary of State, of later Scopes trial fame, whose prohibitionist and fundamentalist religious sentiments were well known. Even so, the bulk of testimony offered to the Senate on behalf of the bill was concerned with international obligations, not with any overt domestic problems.

As enacted by Congress, the Harrison Act was not in any sense a prohibition law. Officially, it was designed to "provide for the registration of, with collectors of internal revenue, and to impose a special tax upon all persons who produce, import, manufacture, compound, deal in, dispense, sell, distribute, or give away, opium or coca leaves, their salts, derivatives or preparations. . . ." The law specifically permitted physicians to prescribe and pharmacists to dispense narcotics. Both were required to keep records of the narcotics they dispensed as their sole accountability to the new law. It was a regulatory measure that was in no way meant to prohibit narcotics.

Then, in what is a tragically common bureaucratic development, the agency charged with enforcement of the act subtly changed both the spirit and the letter of the law. What was originally conceived of and enacted as a regulatory measure became, in fact, a prohibition law—mainly as a result of the zeal and enterprise of the enforcing agencies.

Although the act specifically stated that it was in no way meant to interfere with medical practice—"Nothing contained in this section shall apply to the dispensing or distribution of any of the aforesaid drugs to a patient by a physician, dentist, or veterinary surgeon . . . in the course of his professional practice only"—this last phrase was interpreted by enforcement agencies to mean that no doctor could prescribe narcotics to an addict! Thousands of doctors were persecuted under this provision of the law until addiction was eliminated from medical practice and came solely under the jurisdiction of law enforcement officials.

According to most official estimates, there were more than 1,000,000 people in America who were addicted to opiates at the time the Harrison Act was passed. According to a survey made in 1919, which was cited by Louis Lasagna, MD, in a paper presented before a national Narcotics Conference held at the University of California in April, 1963, 75 percent of all addicts at the time were gainfully employed, and the number included "people of the highest qualities, morally and intellectually, and of great value to their communities."

With the passage of the Harrison Act, however, and the beginning of an almost hysterical enforcement program it became impossible for an addict to live anything approaching a normal life. A full-scale propaganda war was instituted against narcotics, and in sensational news stories, books, lectures, magazine articles, and sermons the evils of addiction were drummed into the American people. In time, the addict came to be looked upon as the "fiend"—the moral degenerate who was beyond the pale of human sympathy or consideration.

A million people who were addicted to narcotics suddenly found themselves without a supply. What happened to them? The great majority of them simply stopped taking the drug. Isidor Chein, PhD, a professor of psychology at New York University, who has worked with addicts for many years, described this transition:

Bear in mind that the Harrison Act was passed in December, 1914, and that its enforcement as a repressive measure did not begin until 1919. Also bear in mind that prior to the Harrison Act opiates not only could be bought legally without prescription, but were common ingredients of over-the-counter proprietary medications. Finally, bear in mind that there is no evidence of any extensive wave of violent reaction by the addicts to the withdrawal of their narcotic supplies. There does not seem to have been a wave of withdrawal sickness or any great upsurge in the number of robberies of pharmacies and physicians' offices . . . the number of addicts was peacefully and quietly reduced. . . .

Although the great majority of addicts were able to manage withdrawal when their regular source of supply was interrupted, there were many who could not control their need. A series of clinics were established for these addicts where they could enter upon a maintenance program under medical supervision. These were soon closed down in response to pressure brought by moralists, and the addicts who were unable to control their need were left on their own. Now the only source of narcotics was illegal smugglers and black marketeers.

These illicit purveyors of drugs had established national and international organizations for the smuggling of drugs within a few years of enforcement of the Harrison Act. In 1921, for example, Dr. A. G. Du Mez, secretary of the Public Health Service, reported on the growing dominance by criminals of the illicit traffic in drugs. He traced a route from Turkey and Iran to Mexico, Canada, and the American market, organized by powerful "hoodlum interests," to bring drugs of questionable quality to addicts.

Dr. Du Mez also noted that the drug of preference among those addicts who bought illegally had become heroin. Indeed, heroin had all but eliminated morphine as the drug of illegal addiction. The reason for this was purely logistic. Heroin is easier to transport than any other form of narcotic. It comes in a powder form that is readily hidden, concentrated, and easily prepared from morphine. As far as pharmacological effects are concerned, heroin and morphine are almost identical, although heroin may be a bit more potent. Addicts in blind tests have been unable to distinguish between the two drugs. Till 1919 the Bayer Company sold a cough remedy whose principal ingredient was heroin to millions of people all over the world!

Still, the concentrated campaign of enforcement and propaganda appeared to have worked. The number of drug addicts declined steadily. In a report to a symposium convened at the National Health Institute, Bethesda, Maryland, in March, 1958, M. L. Harney, superintendent of the Division of Narcotic Control, Illinois State Department of Public Health, recapped the history of addiction in the United States:

. . . Estimates which I believe credible place the narcotic incidence in this country, prior to the early 1920's, at one addict in 200. We saw a steady decline in addiction throughout the 1920's and into the late 1930's. In the 1930's the average age of addicts coming into Lexington was roughly one year older every year. In effect, we had the problem licked. When World War II came along, the traffic was further circumscribed and plummeted to an irreducible minimum. The graph of addiction trend in this country shows essentially a ski-jump profile from the 1920s down to the 1940s when it hits bottom. Then there is a beginning of a rise in 1946–47, then a leveling off about 1951–52, and we hope now a steady decline. . . .

This estimate, of course, was made in the year 1958, when most officials would have agreed with Mr. Harney that the drug problem was all but solved. Alas, this optimism was premature. Along came the 1960's, with their turmoil and change which were felt nowhere as strongly as in the area of drugs. Suddenly, the incidence of addiction leaped forward to create a major social problem.

Programs that were effective in curtailing addiction in the past now were failing dismally. There appeared nothing that the authorities could do to stem the tide short of a complete and radical reevaluation of the situation. One of the great problems was the lack of reliable information. The field of drug addiction had become so confused as to make little sense to anyone seriously considering the problem. Dr. Lawrence Kolb, former superintendent of the Hospital for Drug Addicts at Lexington, Kentucky, describes the state of affairs:

There has been built up in this country an enormous mass of misinformation about the physical and moral effects of addiction. The collectors and disseminators of this misinformation have included sincere laymen and law enforcement officers aided to a considerable extent by otherwise competent physicians. For the most part, these people have exhibited the capacity to generate enthusiasm and zeal for the suppression of vice rather than the desire to obtain and spread proper knowledge of drug addiction. . . . Misinformation about opiates has snow-balled into disaster-producing dimensions in the United States . . . these factual and semantic distortions have led this country to introduce fearful legal and administrative excesses in addiction control.

The problem is that narcotics are highly addicting—people who become addicted must keep taking the drug in order to function in a normal manner. Most addicts suffer painful withdrawal symptoms when drug use is stopped. Here, again, however, there is a great element of exaggeration. Withdrawal symptoms from opiates are generally mild and have little resemblance to the "rolling on the floor, gnashing of teeth, sweating, screaming" depictions seen in the movies.

Beyond the fact of addiction and the withdrawal syndrome, narcotics have very little other effect. They are not toxic; the user does not stagger around like an alcoholic drunk; they have no measurable effect on the character or moral fiber of the user; they do not stimulate the addict to violence; outside of their analgesic effect, opiates do very little. Indeed, on a television program dealing with the subject recently an addict confessed to *an eleven-year history of addiction, during which time he took three intravenous "fixes" every day without raising the suspicion of his employers, fellow workers, or even his family.*

By far the most dangerous and damaging aspect of narcotics addiction stems from the fact of their illegality. Since opiates cannot be purchased legally, the addict is compelled to find sources in the criminal underworld. He must pay an exorbitant price for an uncontrolled product of dangerously variable concentration that often contains poisonous or potentially poisonous adulterants.

Because of the prohibitive sanctions, the addict is in violation of the law simply by being, but his illegality is extended even further by his situation. Black-market prices of illicit drugs put them beyond reach of most legitimate incomes. In order to procure the drug, the addict is driven to unlawful activities, which sooner or later lead to arrest and time spent in prisons. The wealthy addict, of course, can simply buy his supplies and live more or less normally without coming into contact with the law as many thousands do.

In addition to being criminalized by the laws against drugs, the addict is victimized by the nature of the substances he acquires through his criminal contacts. There are no controls on the drugs he buys since they are illegally manufactured and distributed. In the heroin-maintenance program of the streets, the pusher is the physician who creates more addicts to help support his own habit or simply to turn a greater profit. Since the drugs have no quality control, the danger of being poisoned by adulterants is very real, and no one can be held responsible—the addict literally takes his life into his hands every time he injects a dose of illicit drugs. Indeed, most drug deaths, which are generally blamed on overdose, are traced to reactions to adulterants in black-market heroin and other drugs.

Further, the addict is ostracized socially. He is the victim of a sensationalist, misinformed, exaggerated propaganda mill that has pictured him as a "fiend" beyond human redemption. He has been judged a pariah by ordinary citizens, unfit for companionship, regular employment, and generally thought of and treated as a threat to law, order, and social well-being. Those addicts who manage to conceal their habit live in constant fear of being exposed and subjected to the hysterical evaluation of the public and the law.

This, of course, is not meant to suggest that were it not for the law, the typical addict would lead a normal, respectable, and responsible life. This ideal, however, is not as yet required by law. On the other hand, it would be difficult to deny that whatever chance the addict may have had to make something of his life, to live with a modicum of normality, virtually disappears once he becomes addicted. Again, not primarily because of any intrinsic enslavement to the drug—after all, there are tens of millions of Americans who must have their daily cigarettes—but because the addict is using something the mere possession of which and traffic in are subject to vigorous prosecution and harsh penalties. The most partisan people involved in the drug problem will agree that the most damaging aspect of heroin addiction is its illegality!

This is where the situation stands today. In the late 1950's law enforcement officials were congratulating themselves upon their defeat of drug addiction. It seemed, at the time, that the problem had been solved. The incidence of addiction appeared to be growing smaller year by year, and most officials were confident that they would soon all but disappear. Then, beginning in the early 1960's, drug addiction and the sale of illicit heroin skyrocketed. Within ten years the number of addicts increased more than ten times, and there seems to be no end in sight.

At first, heroin addiction appeared to be confined almost exclusively to big-city ghetto areas. This fact of distribution led some black militants to claim that the drug had been deliberately foisted on their communities by the establishment as a means of control and further exploitation. But then incidence of addiction spread to every area of American life. Drug addiction became a national problem, not just a local city ghetto concern.

In response, the authorities increased the number of law enforcement people involved with narcotics, passed harsher laws with more severe penalties for pushers and dealers, and instituted a rash of programs designed to detoxify and rehabilitate addicts—most of which have failed ignobly. In 1973 local, state, and federal government will have spent more than $600,000,000 on enforcement programs, rehabilitation, plus *buying up the entire Turkish crop of opium!*

One of the more successful programs now in vogue is the controversial methadone maintenance technique that is currently treating some 60,000 addicts across the country. In this program, methadone is substituted for heroin. The patient receives a daily dose of methadone together with psychological therapy, job counseling, and other social aids. Methadone is a synthetic opiate developed in Germany during World War II. It is analgesic and highly addictive and is not very different in its effects from heroin.

The addict who enrolls in the methadone maintenance program has the advantage of receiving a drug that is reasonably pure and safe and does not have to pay an exorbitant black-market price. Free from dependence on an illegal source, the addict can, it is hoped, begin to rehabilitate himself. He can try to find a meaningful niche in society once more—a task that is all but impossible while the addict is dependent on illegal heroin. Still, the great drawback to rehabilitation remains the attitude of the public. Because of the sensational distortions that have been saddled upon the addict by irresponsible mass media, it is very difficult for the ex-addict to gain acceptance.

Despite the programs and heralded enforcement campaigns, drug addiction remains an explosive social problem throughout the country. The high profits that accrue to illegal dealing ensures the continued smuggling of drugs. Nor can wholesale suppression of cultivation of the opium poppy help. The main drawback here is that the plant will grow practically anywhere. Eliminate the production in Turkey, for example, and cultivation will merely shift to another area. Laos, Thailand,

and Vietnam now appear to be developing into major supply areas for the opium trade. We cannot hope to police the whole world!

Actually, the problem is not opium (or heroin, or hashish, or any other drug) in itself, but our attitudes toward drugs. So long as our approach to the problem is based on hysteria, self-righteousness, and a "sin" concept, so long will the problem remain. Our main task in relation to the "white plague" is to try to approach the problem rationally and with intelligence—something we have never yet attempted. If we can succeed, the problem will not seem to be unsolvable.

7. THE HALLUCINOGE[NS]

THIS is a class of drugs that is as ancient as any known to man. In processes that are still only vaguely understood, these substances react on the nerves and brain to alter sense perceptions and trigger hallucinatory experiences. They occur naturally in a variety of plants and fungi that grow all over the world. No one can say for certain when men first discovered the mind-altering properties of these drugs, but we do know that it happened far back in time all over the world. Actually, even animals are drawn to plants and fungi that affect their moods and nervous systems.

Ranging from the laurel leaves, whose burning vapors were ingested by the priestess at Delphi in ancient Greece to induce prophetic trance, to the "magic" mushrooms eaten by Indian shamans and priests to achieve heightened spiritual awareness in Mexico and our Southwest, these drugs have always been closely associated with mysticism and the religious experience.

So close has this identification been historically that some scholars have linked hallucinogenic drugs with the origin of religion. William James in his book *The Varieties of Religious*

Experience, for example, suggests that the sense of heightened awareness that some drugs create in the user may have revealed the possibility of a richer potentiality in life than that which is available under ordinary consciousness. This possibility, James argues, along with the wonder and awe generated by a bewildering and complex universe and the mysteries posed by the cycles of life and death, generation and degeneration, may have been among the primary sources of the religious impulse in early man.

In America, this class of drugs has a particularly venerable history. Like the pumpkin and potato, we can think of them as native. As we have already seen, the people who inhabited North and South America developed an elaborate and highly sophisticated pharmacopoeia of psychedelic drugs long before the arrival of Europeans. Almost all the nations and tribes of the New World utilized these drugs as medicines, for recreational purposes, and as religious sacraments.

The one exception was the Eskimo of the far north, who, before the introduction of alcohol by Europeans, had no experience with drugs. Eskimos had to rely on chants and dances to achieve mystic trance states. All the naturally occurring hallucinogens come from either plants or fungi. In the frigid Arctic areas inhabited by the Eskimos few plants grew and their diet was limited almost exclusively to meat and fish.

Archaeological findings indicate that psychedelic cults flourished in Guatemala and southern Mexico some 3,500 years ago. Stone carvings, reliefs, and decorated pottery depicting religious rites that centered on the ritual eating of mushrooms were discovered in a number of such ancient sites. The practice described on these artifacts has continued without interruption to this day.

Spanish chroniclers who accompanied the legions that conquered Mexico and South America, for example, wrote detailed descriptions of a mushroom cult among the highly civilized Aztecs of Mexico. In one of their most solemn rituals, a mushroom called teonanacatl was solemnly ingested by all the participants celebrating the rite as the principal sacrament.

The name teonanacatl is translated to mean "flesh of the God." The similarity between this rite of a pagan Aztec people to Catholic practice is striking, and Spanish priests came to look on this ceremony as a diabolical caricature of the Catholic mass. In the sacrament of communion, Catholics eat the flesh and drink the blood of Jesus and thus all communicants are united to become part of the mystic body of Christ—the Catholic Church—on earth.

The Aztec mushroom sacrament had an identical symbolic meaning to its communicants and held an equally sacred status in their religious life. In the Aztec practice, however, the participants experienced a mystic trance induced by the hallucinogenic properties of the mushrooms they ingested. Probably the wine originally served in earlier Catholic communion rites may have been utilized for the same reasons.

Ritual ingestion of hallucinogenic mushrooms continues to this day among the Indians of Mexico and Central America. Such practices were reported by the botanists R. Gordon Wasson and Roger Heim during a field trip to Mexico and Guatemala in 1954. During a later trip, Dr. Wasson participated in one such rite. The ritual he described was almost identical to that seen by Spanish writers 300 years earlier. Unlike the Spanish historians, however, Dr. Wasson sampled the mushrooms and described the vivid hallucinations he experienced after eating twelve of them in a paper published in a book titled *The Drug Takers*:

> The visions were in vivid color, always harmonious. They began with angular art motifs, such as might decorate carpets or wallpaper or the drawing board of an architect. Then they evolved into palaces with courts, arcades, gardens—resplendent palaces all laid over with semiprecious stones . . . then it was as though the walls of our house had dissolved and my spirit flew forth and I was suspended in mid-air viewing towering landscapes of mountains, with camel caravans advancing slowly across wide slopes. . . . I saw mythological beasts drawing regal chariots . . . sharply focused, the lines and colors seemed more real to me than anything I had ever seen with my own eyes. . . .

One of the most significant aspects of the experience, Dr. Wasson wrote, was the sense of kinship he felt toward all the other participants in the ceremony during and immediately following the height of the drug effect. He felt as though his own ego had dissolved and merged with that of the others who had ingested the bitter-tasting mushrooms with him.

Although this type of ritual ingestion of hallucinogens was widespread among the Indian population of both North and South America, the practice had comparatively little impact on European settlers in the New World. Alcohol, of course, was their drug of choice. More immediately intoxicating than any of the psychedelics, with an effect that was neither subtle nor ambiguous, alcohol dominated the drug life of the early settlers of the Western Hemisphere.

Tobacco, of course, was the main exception. This highly addicting drug was taken up by Europeans and everyone else introduced to it with bewildering enthusiasm. Tobacco spread through the world with a rapidity and thoroughness that still amaze us to this day. Within fifty years of the discovery of Columbus, tobacco had circled the globe and was used everywhere.

With this exception, the psychedelic drugs used by most of the Indian peoples had no appreciable impact on colonial and early American society. This neglect is not difficult to understand. Since "might made right," it was obvious that European culture in all aspects, including drug preference, was superior to anything that the "savage and barbaric" natives of the New World could offer. Hallucinogenic drugs and the psychedelic experience were central to Indian religious and tribal life; *ergo*, there was something inherently sinister and diabolic about these practices. No self-respecting white man would think of indulging them.

With the remorseless attrition of the Indian population, the use of hallucinogenic drugs in America waned and almost disappeared. The use of these drugs was part of the life pattern of a people who were being systematically destroyed by an "advanced" European culture.

Within 150 years of the landing of the Pilgrims at Plymouth Rock—in search of religious freedom—the tribes of the eastern seaboard were destroyed as viable social organizations. The destruction did not stop there. It followed in the wake of the continued westward migration of European settlers. The dreamers of the forests, mountains, and prairies could not stand up to the forward march of the Europeans. This alien people had perfected the arts and techniques of war to an extent that the Indians could not even conceive.

By the end of the nineteenth century the American Indians were a shattered people. Pushed off their lands, the game they depended on wantonly massacred, they found the fabric of their lives irrevocably torn. The remnants of a proud and dignified people who lacked the European capacity for war and destruction were relegated to reservations as wards of a more often than not corrupt Bureau of Indian Affairs. Their defeat and humiliation were complete.

It was in this atmosphere of despair that a new impulse of religious fervor gripped this sad remnant of a people. One of the prime movers in this revival was Quannah Parker, a Comanche chief and a renowned warrior. Quannah Parker realized that his people could not stop the flow of encroaching whites that moved westward in a flood after the Civil War. Recognizing approaching doom, Quannah Parker went alone into the wilderness to seek a guiding vision in the ancient Indian fashion.

After fasting and meditating for many weeks, the Comanche warrior experienced the vision he had sought. The Great Spirit of the Land appeared and spoke to him, outlining a new religion and a ritual that would unite and save the dispersed and defeated Indian remnants:

Lay down your arms, Quannah Parker. Your solution, as is the solution of all creatures, is personal. Turn your energies toward conquering the self. Only through this will you and your people have a freedom which exceeds that of the white man's. I have planted my flesh in the cactus pioniyo [peyote]. Partake of it as it is the food of your soul. Through it you will continue to communicate with me. When all Red men are united by pioniyo, then and only then will they once again reign supreme over their lands. The white civilizations will destroy themselves and the Indian will return to nature, master over himself and at peace with all.

This was the message that Quannah Parker brought back to his people from his vigil in the wilderness, together with a ritual that combined peyote and prayer and formed the basis of a new religion that swept through what was left of the Indian nations of North America. By the beginning of the twentieth century the cult of peyotism had penetrated all the tribes of the Great Plains from Mexico to Canada.

In the peyote ritual, as practiced by the members of the Native American Church, the sacrament is prepared by cutting off the tops, or buttons, of the peyote plant, slicing them into thin disks which are dried in the sun. The dried disks either are boiled in water to make a tea or are eaten as they are during the ceremony. When eaten, the disks are chewed until softened and swallowed. The peyote buttons have a bitter taste that is strong enough to induce nausea in people who are not accustomed to the flavor.

The peyote ceremony is long, lasting from sunset to sunrise. Meetings are generally called to deal with specific problems that arise among members. Sickness, emotional distress, and alcoholism suffered by a member or a friend or relative are the most common situations that call for a meeting. The ritual is directed by a leader assisted by several adepts, although this direction is not obvious and all those present at the ceremony take turns in leading different aspects.

The principal function of the leaders, or road chiefs, is to control the effects of the drug that is ingested at the ceremony. If a participant should become withdrawn, as one example, the road chief brings him back into active participation with the group. Road chiefs, however, are not a professional clergy. All work at other occupations and participate in the peyote ceremony as a sacred service to the members. These adepts learn their role through an apprenticeship that lasts six or seven years before they are considered qualified to lead a ceremony.

Those celebrating the rite usually sit in a circle around a central altar or fireplace. The ceremony is organized around a sequence of ritual events much as a Catholic mass is celebrated. Singing and chanting to the accompaniment of drums and gourd rattles are important parts of the ceremony that are led by each participant in turn. At specific points in the service, peyote is passed around the circle, and each member is free to take as much as he wants. This passing out of the drug is repeated several times during the night.

Everything in the rite appears to be designed to heighten the sense of togetherness generated among the participants. They sing together, pray together, and partake of the peyote buttons together. The main emphasis of the meeting is a kind of group therapy that observers report as being very effective. Participants simply discuss their problems, and the group attempts to work out solutions.

At one such meeting observed by J. S. Slotkin and described in his book *The Peyote Religion*, the meeting was called to help in an alcoholic problem suffered by a relative of a regular member who had brought him to the meeting. All the participants described their own feelings toward drinking and the methods they had used to control the problem. The man suffering from alcoholism was made to feel part of the group. He realized that his problem was a common one and one that could be solved. In the group discussion, all offered advice, and all had an opportunity to learn.

This idea of learning is a fundamental aspect of the peyote ritual. Mr. Slotkin spoke to an elderly Indian who had participated in the cult for all his adult life. He spoke of the importance of learning:

Some of them, they say that the great teacher Peyote teaches forever. That's the way they find out, the peyoters, old peyoters. Even next meeting I go, I'll find something; next one, I'll find something. Keep on going like that; you'll never get to end. There's no end to it; it is forever.

When the peyote religion first spread through the reservations where the surviving Indian population was confined, the reaction of the Bureau of Indian Affairs, predictably, was to forbid the use of the drug and make possession of peyote a crime. Oklahoma, for example, passed a law in 1899 making any use of peyote a criminal offense. This law, however, was repealed in 1908, after Chief Quannah Parker, one of the originators of the cult, testified before a legislative committee.

New Mexico, Montana, Arizona, Nevada, and Utah all passed laws that outlawed the use of peyote during the same period. Most of these laws have since been either repealed or ignored. Today the use of peyote as a sacrament in religious ceremonies conducted by members of the Native American Church is legal. This ritual use of the drug is recognized as a valid religious practice, and as such peyote comes under constitutional religious guarantees.

With the exception of the ritual use of psychedelic drugs by the Indians, there was apparently little other use of significance by the rest of the population of the United States until the mid-twentieth century. Of course, the dramatic mind-altering effects of peyote and other hallucinogenic drugs were of clinical interest to doctors and psychiatrists, but they never caught the fancy of the general population. Havelock Ellis, the famed English physician and sexologist, for example, sampled peyote in 1898 and left a vivid description of the experience in his journal:

> . . . the visions never resembled familiar objects; they
> were extremely definite, but yet always novel; they were
> constantly approaching, and yet constantly eluding the
> semblance of known things. I would see thick, glorious fields
> of jewels, solitary or clustered, sometimes brilliant and
> sparkling, sometimes with a dull rich glow. Then they would
> spring up into gorgeous butterfly forms or endless folds of
> glistening, iridescent, fibrous wings of wonderful insects. . . .
> I was surprised, not only by the enormous profusion of
> imagery presented to my gaze, but still more by its vari-
> ety. . . .

Until its sale was made illegal to the public in 1965, peyote
could be bought by anyone in America who was interested. A
number of companies in Texas, Arizona, and New Mexico
collected and sold dried peyote buttons and shipped them all
over the country. Advertisements for the sale of peyote
appeared in magazines and newspapers throughout America.
The going price in 1950 was $8 for 100 buttons—4 or 5 had to
be eaten to trigger a psychedelic experience.

Although peyote was available and comparatively inexpensive, few people took advantage of this opportunity. There
were always some who experimented with the drug, and the
companies that supplied peyote filled a steady, if unspectacu-
lar, demand. Certainly, nothing remotely resembling a problem was connected with this sale. Then Aldous Huxley
published a book titled *Doors of Perception* that was destined to
exert a major influence on the drug life of America.

Already a distinguished writer with a score of novels and
essays to his credit, Huxley described his experiences with
mescaline in glowing terms. Mescaline is the active ingredient
of peyote that was first identified by Ludwig Lewin, a German
pharmacologist, in 1886.

Huxley compared his reaction to the drug with the mystic states achieved by adepts of Eastern religions after arduous periods of training and preparation. Mescaline, in Huxley's view, offered an access to these exalted states that was open to all. He saw the psychedelic experience as a vital source of personal development, growth, and liberation.

This remarkable book had an undeniable influence on the subsequent growth in the use of hallucinogenic drugs in America. In the year 1954 the country was ready for this kind of influence. A half century earlier Dr. Havelock Ellis, also a distinguished and influential writer and thinker, said the same things about the drug in his reports, but outside of whetting the curiosity of his fellow doctors and a few readers, his book had little further effect.

Aldous Huxley's descriptions of the psychedelic experience triggered a flood of followers. In the mid-1950's strange things were beginning to happen in America. The whole country appeared to be changing its head—a process that came to a peak in the 1960's, when it became obvious that a revolution in the drug habits of America was taking place.

Word of the fascination afforded by the psychedelic experience spread, and the use of hallucinogenic drugs grew steadily. At first, this use was limited to a bohemian fringe of artists, poets, and visionaries. Allen Ginsberg, for example, wrote feelingly about the psychedelic experience, and what came to be known as the beat poets enthusiastically followed suit. When the price of peyote buttons leapfrogged in response to growing demand in the late 1950's, the rise provided a reliable index to the popularity of the psychedelic experience.

At the same time, another drug was beginning to command increased attention. This drug, of course, was LSD—a hallucinogenic that is so potent that dosages are measured in micrograms (millionths of a gram) and an amount sufficient to trigger the most profound effects can barely be seen by the naked eye.

LSD is a comparatively new drug. It was first synthesized in the spring of 1938 at the Sandoz Laboratories, near Basel, Switzerland. Dr. Albert Hofmann, a chemist and an officer of the company, together with his assistant, Dr. Arthur Stoll, were conducting a series of experiments with synthesizing a number of compounds derived from ergot.

Ergot (*Claviceps purpurea*), a parasitic fungus that grows on rye and other grains, was known for centuries for its mysterious properties. European midwives used it to assist in childbirth and in the performance of abortions. Small doses of the fungus were known both to alleviate pain and to stop bleeding. It was also known that ergot sometimes produced visual and mental aberrations, and entire villages that had ingested ergot-tainted bread experienced group hallucinations. In medieval times, of course, these were explained as visitations of the devil.

The Sandoz company, beginning in 1935, had synthesized several ergot-related compounds that it marketed as aids in childbirth. One of these drugs was widely used to induce uterine contractions after childbirth. Another was used as a treatment for migraine headaches. Dr. Hofmann and Dr. Stoll were searching for other ergot-derived medicines. D-lysergic acid diethylamide tartate was the twenty-fifth compound synthesized in this series. Since there was no immediate use for the compound, LSD 25 was put on the shelf along with the first twenty-four ergot compounds.

Then, five years later, on April 16, 1943, Dr. Hofmann accidentally ingested a minute dose of the compound. This first recorded reaction to the drug was reported in the Swiss *Archives of Neurology*:

> Last Friday on the 16th of April I had to leave my work in the laboratory and go home because I felt strangely restless and dizzy. I got home, lay down and sank into a not unpleasant delirium which was characterized by an extreme degree of fantasy (a kind of trance). I kept my eyes closed because I found the daylight very unpleasant. Fantastic visions of extraordinary vividness accompanied by a kaleidoscopic-like play of intense coloration continually swirled around my head. The condition lasted for about two hours.

Dr. Hofmann deliberately took the drug again a few days later to confirm its effects. The results were unmistakable. A minute amount of LSD 25—250 micrograms—was enough to trigger hallucinatory effects. Again, this information had little practical effect. LSD was put back on the shelf for another five years. Apparently no practical use could be found for this remarkably potent drug.

The next step in this history came in 1947, when the son of Dr. Hofmann's assistant, Dr. W. A. Stoll, a medical doctor and psychiatrist, obtained a batch of the drug, which he administered to both normal volunteers and mental patients. Dr. Stoll was able to confirm in detail the reactions first experienced by Dr. Hofmann. He also discovered that as little as 30 micrograms of the drug would trigger reactions.

The first shipment of LSD to the United States was made in 1949, when a quantity of the drug was sent to Dr. Max Rinkel of the Massachusetts Mental Health Center. Dr. Rinkel had read about the experiments conducted by Dr. Stoll in Switzerland. He administered the drug to some 100 volunteers at the New England center and confirmed the results of European researchers. Dr. Rinkel, however, was struck by the remarkable similarity in mental processes exhibited by LSD-influenced subjects to some of the delusions of schizophrenics.

After Dr. Rinkel's findings were published, a great deal of interest in the properties of the drug was generated. Here was a substance that temporarily created many of the symptoms of nervous disorders. Perhaps it could be helpful in understanding the elusive mechanisms of schizophrenia.

In the early fifties, LSD was used in hospitals and laboratories all over America as an experimental tool. Not only was the drug administered to normal volunteers and mental patients, but it was also given to a variety of animals with strange results. Under the influence of LSD some spiders built more elaborate webs than they would ordinarily. Sheep used in experiments were found to pace about in repetitive patterns that consisted of circles, ovals, and figure eights. Rats became more passive after administration of the drug, and some exhibited spatial disorientation under its influence.

The United States Army tested the drug for possible use in chemical warfare or as an aid in brainwashing or a method for inducing prisoners to reveal information. For a time, large amounts of LSD were stockpiled by the Army Chemical Corps for possible use in disabling an enemy. Since that time, however, the military has developed far more effective mind-altering drugs, and its interest in LSD has been superseded.

Between the years 1949, when LSD was introduced to the United States, and 1965, when use of the drug was declared illegal, the potent compound was used experimentally in a variety of contexts. LSD was administered to normal volunteers, mental patients, alcoholics, criminals, heroin addicts, scholars, housewives, slow learners and fast learners, plus a Noah's Ark full of animals.

In psychotherapy, it proved a useful, if unpredictable, tool. It appeared to be effective in the treatment of alcoholics and heroin addicts, although the experiments in these areas were not conclusive. LSD treatment also proved beneficial in some areas of criminal mentality—it appeared to offer the participant an insight into sources of antisocial behavior. It was as a recreational drug, however, that the full notoriety of LSD was manifested.

As was to be expected, the first people to use LSD recreationally were the physicians, psychiatrists, and other mental health professionals who had used it in their work. Many of them had volunteered to ingest the drug and had found the effects pleasurable or enlightening and continued its use outside the laboratory and clinic. Professional use of LSD was thus extended to their private lives, and they introduced it to interested friends. By the mid-1950's America received its first reports of LSD being used recreationally for nontherapeutic purposes.

In a book, *Utopiates: The Use and Users of LSD-25*, prepared by Dr. Richard H. Blum, a psychologist at Stanford University, and his associates, the early recreational use of the drug was described. Through in-depth interviews of almost 100 nonmedical users of LSD, the study attempted to trace the effects on these early users. Some of the statements made were guaranteed to generate controversy:

> Everyone reported pleasant reactions or "kicks"—being "high" or having "freedom from troubles" . . . some of the sample also spoke of their mystical religious experiences and most described unusual feelings of closeness and special

appreciation of others. Upon occasion, we were told, these interpersonal delights became quite specific as the partying people took off their clothes and played romantic roulette.

Before the 1960's hardly anyone in America had ever heard about LSD. For all effects and purposes, it remained an interesting, staggeringly potent mind-affecting drug that had potential value in the treatment of some mental problems. All the LSD distributed to the profession was manufactured by Sandoz Laboratories. Within a few years, however, LSD was to leap out of the laboratory and clinic in a flood that threatened to send the entire country on an "acid trip."

No one had more of an influence upon the growing notoriety of LSD than a doctor of clinical psychology, named Timothy Leary, who was on the staff of the Harvard University Center for Research in Personality. In the summer of 1960 Dr. Leary vacationed in Mexico. At the villa of a friend in Cuernavaca, where he was staying with his two children, Leary heard about a mushroom used by local Indians that had far-reaching mental effects.

His interest piqued, Leary obtained some mushrooms from an old Indian lady known as Crazy Jane who lived in the mountains a few miles from town, according to his own accounts. The story, however, may be apocryphal. "Crazy Jane" was the prophetic lady of the famous Yeats poems, and the similarity in name may not have been coincidental. Anyway, Leary chewed on the mushrooms one pleasant afternoon next to the pool. This act, he later wrote, proved to be a turning point in his life and career. The psychedelic experience triggered by the mushrooms had a profound effect. The psychologist realized then that "the old Timothy Leary was dead" and that his Timothy Leary "game" was over.

After returning to Harvard in the fall of 1960, Dr. Leary began a systematic investigation of hallucinogenic drugs and the psychedelic experience. He was joined in this work by a fellow faculty member, Dr. Richard Alpert, who was also on the staff of the research center. The two psychologists instituted a study of psilocybin, the active ingredient of the hallucinogenic mushrooms Leary had ingested in Mexico, which had been synthesized in 1959 by the Sandoz Laboratories; mescaline; and LSD—the most potent hallucinogen of them all. They conferred and worked closely with the late Aldous Huxley, who was then in residence at the nearby Massachusetts Institute of Technology.

One of their first studies involved thirty-five prisoners at the Massachusetts Correctional Institute at Concord. They wanted to learn whether the psychedelic experience might be able to provide their subjects with meaningful insights into their antisocial attitudes and behavior. In carrying out this study, both psychologists became dissatisfied with the traditional detachment that the experimenter is expected to maintain toward his subjects. Leary and Alpert came to rely heavily on close personal relationships which they developed with their prisoner subjects.

Although a significant percentage of the convicts treated by Leary and Alpert showed positive results and managed to stay out of courts and prisons after being released, in comparison with those who did not participate in the experiment, this success was not greeted with any degree of enthusiasm by their colleagues. The two psychologists had broken too many rules. For one thing, they had entered into close personal relationships with their convict subjects and had not maintained a respectable professional distance. For another, they had administered drugs in many instances without the presence of medical doctors.

Their unorthodox approach, however, had evolved out of experience with psychedelic drugs. One of the first things that Leary and Alpert noticed was the extreme variation in response to an identical drug in different people and even the same people under differing physical and psychological conditions. This observation led to the discovery of the importance of what they termed "set" and "setting" when dealing with any mind-altering drug.

"Set" is defined as the total mental attitude that a subject brings to a drug, encompassing personal expectations, the subject's ideas about how the drug will affect him, and his individual reflection of the general attitude toward the drug that prevails in society as a whole.

A good example of the importance of set in the action of a drug is provided by the bizarre history of ether. When ether was introduced as a general anesthetic in the mid-1850's, it proved ineffective in many cases. In many people, administration failed to induce anesthesia. Today the same compound is considered one of medicine's most reliable anesthetics. In his book *The Natural Mind* Dr. Andrew Weil explains this paradox: "Today, a very powerful set exists among surgical patients that ether and other anesthetic gases will cause unconsciousness."

People expect to be anesthetized by ether—this is their set—and they are! Dr. Weil goes on to probe into the state of anesthesia itself as induced by administration of ether and concludes that this profound trance is actually an altered state of consciousness: "If, after recovery from an operation, a patient is hypnotized, he may be able to quote word for word conversations that went on while he was 'asleep' on the operating table."

"Setting" refers to the physical and social environment in which a drug is taken. In their experiments, Leary and Alpert noted the extreme variation with which subjects reacted to the same drug, ranging from no noticeable effect to the most profound mental changes and manifestations. After a long series of tests and trials, the two doctors concluded that set and setting were the principal controlling elements in these varied reactions to drug administration.

Convinced that the sterile, clinical surroundings of the laboratory had a negative effect on the drug experience, Leary began to hold sessions at his own home where more sympathetic conditions could be maintained. Appropriate music and lights, incense, and comfortable couches and chairs together with imaginative decorations became part of the Leary experimental environment.

Word of the experiments conducted by Leary and Alpert spread over the Harvard campus, and it seemed that practically the entire undergraduate student body was ready to volunteer. Between 1961 and 1963 the two psychologists administered hallucinogenic drugs to more than 400 volunteer subjects. They came to see the psychedelic experience as more than just an interesting mental experience, but as a vital character-shaping force. Their work, however, came into increasing conflict with school officials.

The conflict was not aided by the growing publicity that came to surround LSD and the work of Drs. Leary and Alpert. Probably no drug in history received the exposure in the mass media that the hallucinogens were subjected to during this period. On the one hand, a cult with religious overtones had developed over the psychedelic experience which was seen by its advocates as a cure for all the ills of man and society. Accounts written by "acid trippers" vied with one another to report more ecstatic, more imaginative, more meaningful drug experiences. According to some of them, it would seem that the gates of paradise had been opened at last to all.

The authorities, on the other hand, suspecting a new source of illicit pleasure, a new "kick" that might encourage youth to stray from "proper" social pathways, screamed for blood! In smoke-filled rooms and at martini-spiked conferences the police, government officials, and politicians came to the conclusion that the "psychedelic" experience was criminal. Reports about the alleged dangers of LSD were widely circulated. The result was predictable: By 1964, when the first anti-LSD laws were being enacted, millions of Americans had *tripped* on the drug.

At that time, it must be remembered, there were no reports of any damage done by either LSD or any of the other hallucinogens to anybody. There were, however, a rash of sensational stories about the effects of these drugs. Timothy Leary, who had been expelled from Harvard in May, 1963, along with Dr. Alpert, did nothing to cool matters. An interview published in *Playboy* magazine sometime later was typical. In it, Dr. Leary described LSD as the most powerful aphrodisiac ever known. He went on to say that sex, while under the influence of the drug, was an ecstatic experience that was so superior to ordinary sex as to fall into a different category—a statement not designed to pacify "uptight" authority, to say the least.

In response to these and other similar reports, LSD and all similar drugs, whether synthetic or natural, were declared illegal. A law introduced into the New York legislature in

1964 was passed in 1965. It provided for two-year penalties for "possession, sale, exchange, or giving away" any hallucinogen without a special license.

Finally, in late 1965 and early 1966, two incidents involving LSD made the headlines. In one of them, a five-year-old girl in Brooklyn swallowed an LSD-impregnated sugar cube stored in the refrigerator by her young uncle. When the girl told her family that she had eaten the sugar cube, her parents rushed her to a hospital, where the girl's stomach was promptly pumped. Several doctors argued that this was a useless measure since the drug had already entered the bloodstream and that the painful operation was probably more disturbing to the child than the drug. The girl recovered from the experience, however, and appeared to suffer no permanent damage.

The second incident was more serious. In this case a thirty-two-year-old man was charged with the brutal slaying of his mother-in-law. When apprehended, the man claimed that he had been so "high" on LSD that he could remember nothing. Newspapers and police immediately branded the case as the "LSD Murder." As it turned out, the man had a long history of mental disturbance and was found not guilty by reason of insanity. The question of LSD was not even raised at the trial.

These two events, however, triggered a frenetic drive for additional anti-LSD legislation. The original law passed in 1965 was amended in 1966 to raise the penalty from a maximum of two years to twenty years for "possession, sale, exchange or giving away" LSD. In a typical reaction, the Speaker of the New York Assembly, A. J. Travia, deemed that the problem was so urgent that he would put off all hearings on the law until after the law was passed!

Naturally, these same two events were cited in various other states, including California and Maryland, as arguments in favor of their LSD legislation. The effect of this legislation was almost immediate: The price of LSD trebled, and illicit manufacturers sprang up to supply a demand with questionable products. The use of the drug increased spectacularly all over the country.

Meanwhile, Dr. Timothy Leary, who had been hounded out of Harvard because of his advocacy of the psychedelic experience, continued to have his troubles with the authorities. He moved to Mexico, where he set up an establishment for psychedelic experimentation. The Mexican authorities soon evicted him from this haven, and Leary returned to America, where he set up shop in upstate New York. Shortly after, local police raided the premises after claiming to have witnessed "people acting differently . . . dancing wildly around a bonfire and that's not normal."

The thirty state and local policemen who staged the raid found a bag of marijuana on the premises. Leary, however, denied knowledge of any illegal drugs. Explaining the events to a reporter later, Leary asked, "You don't expect that thirty policemen could search this house for five hours without finding marijuana, do you?"

Finally, Timothy Leary was jailed on a charge of bringing marijuana into the country from Mexico. A Supreme Court decision freed him when they ruled that parts of the law under which he was imprisoned were unconstitutional. He was rearrested almost immediately and retried and reindicted on the same charge. Leary later escaped from prison and fled to North Africa and then to Europe. He has since returned to the United States, where he is now serving time in Folsom Prison in California.

Today, after a widely publicized chromosome scare proved groundless, the LSD hysteria has subsided somewhat. Possession and sale still remain a crime, and in New York former Governor Nelson Rockefeller lumped LSD together with heroin, cocaine, and hashish as "hard drugs" which he proposed to control by imposing mandatory life sentences on all who "deal or give them away." Despite the laws, however, the use of LSD and other hallucinogens remains widespread—one of the staples of America's drug revolution.

We have come to realize that LSD is not the promised door to an earthly paradise, but neither is it the menace seen by most authorities. The anti-LSD publicity, the hysterical scare campaigns, and the laws all helped change this drug from a relatively unknown laboratory tool into a notorious "hard drug." Although the use of this drug appears to have abated somewhat, it remains one of the principal drug experiences of today's campus and youth scene. It does not seem likely that this situation will change. LSD can be too easily synthesized by clandestine laboratories, and a little bit goes such a long, long way.

8. OUT OF THE TEST TUBE

NOT very many years ago, the purveyor of drugs was a special person with a vast knowledge of plants, herbs, and spices. He or she was generally older, or at least this is the picture that comes to mind, and was almost always associated with healing and religion in an unconventional sense. He was familiar with secret plants and herbs. He could prepare a draft that could ease the pain of childbirth, help a distraught farmer sleep, or bring relief to an arthritis-twisted limb. He mixed potions that might bring love or revenge. Drug purveyors were country midwives and herbalists. They were healers. At times, they were called witches and warlocks. There was something uncanny about them. Their secret knowledge evoked a sense of veneration and fear.

When we go back a bit farther in history, we come to a time when physician, priest, and purveyor of drugs were one and the same person. Drugs, religion, and healing were entwined into a single mystic facet of human existence. Among the American Indians, as one example, these three functions were centered on one figure: the witch doctor or shaman. He or she—there were examples from both sexes—was a central and respected personage in tribal hierarchy. The shaman was responsible for both the bodies and souls of the tribe.

The witch doctor was physician and herbalist. He—or she—was expected to be able to set a broken bone, be familiar with those herbs that could still the burning fever, as well as the potions that would induce the guiding vision and mystic ecstasy that were central to the Indian's rich and elaborate religious life. The shaman was source of wisdom and tribal lore and the final arbiter of arguments and disagreements.

A shaman was called to the work. Not everyone could qualify for this demanding profession. The would-be shaman had to demonstrate natural ability as both priest and healer before being admitted to apprenticeship. Training was long and arduous, and most who embarked on this discipline failed. The accolyte had to master an elaborate lore of plants and herbs; he had to learn tribal mysteries and myths and recite them at appropriate ceremonies; he had to be a physician and master psychologist with a deep understanding of the people he was to serve. More important than all this, he had to be master of himself.

The tradition of priest-physician-drug purveyor as one person occurred in practically all societies in the past. Indeed, it is only during the past century or so that this tradition has faded from Christian practice. The wise old monk who gathered plants and herbs from forest and field and combined them into wondrous medicines and potions is not far from living memory. Not only did the monk-physician cure the ills of the body, but he also heard confessions and ministered to the needs of the soul.

It was a kindly, sympathetic monk who came to the aid of the star-crossed lovers and prepared the draft that would simulate Juliet's death, in Shakespeare's *Romeo and Juliet.* This tradition of Catholic priest-physician-drug purveyor is echoed in today's production of liquors, brandies, and wines by monkish orders that are still part of the Catholic Church. They remind us that body and soul were once a single whole that was the province of a single discipline.

In today's modern, compartmentalized world, body and soul have been split asunder. What had always been a comfortable and manageable whole has been divided up among specialists. The priest ministers to the soul, the physician is in charge of the body, while the drug purveyor has been relegated to the netherworld.

In this new lexicon of responsibility the purveyor of drugs has fared most poorly. He is the fallen angel in both his guises, the personification of evil. As pusher he is corrupter and defiler, an object of loathing and detestation for whom even death is not punishment enough. As white-smocked scientist, working in mysterious laboratories, he has not fared better. In this guise he is the diabolical seeker after forbidden knowledge: "There are things that man was not meant to know, Dr. Frankenstein."

This change is most recent and had its beginnings at the turn of the century, but did not come into full flower until the years following World War II. Within the past twenty years, patents have been issued for more than 12,000 mind-affecting drugs, and the list grows daily.

Basically, there are three types of psycho-active drugs: stimulants, depressants, and hallucinogens. All three occur in nature. Cocaine is a natural stimulant; alcohol and opiates are depressants; and mescaline and psilocybin are examples of hallucinogens.

Artificially synthesized drugs developed in laboratories by

chemists and pharmacologists have surpassed nature in variety and effectiveness. LSD, as one example, is far more potent than any hallucinogen that occurs in nature. Synthetic drugs can be tailored to specific needs and purposes. Combinations and permutations of entire spectra of laboratory-produced stimulants and depressants can be harmonized with precise control.

Among the first synthetic drugs were ether and nitrous oxide (laughing gas). Ether is the older of the two, having been first produced by Friedrich Hoffmann, a German physician and chemist. Hoffmann introduced ether to medicine under the name "anodyne" in 1730 and recommended it to "alleviate the pains of kidney stones, gallstones, intestinal cramps, toothache, earache and painful menstruation."

It is interesting to note that although ether was introduced as a medicine useful in the relief of pain, it was used recreationally before it came into widespread use as an anesthetic. In northern Ireland ether came to rival alcohol as the favorite intoxicant. The practice began in 1840 when a great temperance campaign was instituted in Ireland. So effective was the preaching of the leaders of this crusade that thousands of alcoholics took the pledge. At the same time, a heavy tax placed on all alcoholic beverages made them too expensive for casual indulgence by most people.

One of the people who took the pledge during this temperance crusade was a physician in Draperstown, in northern Ireland. The doctor discovered that ether had much the same effect as alcohol, and since he had sworn off the evil brew, he could imbibe the new intoxicant without breaking his word. Soon the doctor's practice became common knowledge, and the whole town appeared to go on an ether binge.

Actually, ether had many advantages. It was inexpensive,

and its action was quick. Moreover, there were no aftereffects, no painful hangovers to contend with. An ether drunk lasted only an hour or so and could be repeated several times during a day. The practice became so popular that a surgeon visiting northern Ireland in 1878 remarked that the towns smelled like his surgery—they were so full of the fumes of ether.

Nitrous oxide was discovered by the English chemist Joseph Priestley in 1772, and its anesthetic properties were described in 1799 by Sir Humphry Davy. Sir Humphry also suggested that the gas be used for surgical operations. This suggestion, however, was not developed at the time. Instead, nitrous oxide came into favor as an intoxicant. In colleges and universities in England and America, laughing gas was used by students much as LSD and marijuana were to be used a century later.

One enterprising American medical student, Gardner Quincy Colton, made laughing gas his profession. After having sampled nitrous oxide at school, young Colton recognized its commercial possibilities. He quit medical school and toured America with a demonstration of the gas in theaters and lecture halls. His advertisements promised entertaining "diversions as volunteers fall under the influence of nitrous oxide and laugh, sing, dance, speak according to the leading trait of their character." In order to make the entertainment "in every respect a genteel affair," the gas would be administered only to gentlemen of first respectability.

A young dentist named Horace Wells attended Colton's demonstration in Hartford, Connecticut. Wells was greatly impressed when one of the laughing gas sniffers tripped and fell on the stair leading to the stage. Although the victim suffered a severe cut on his leg, he reportedly did not feel any pain. Intrigued, Wells, who had been suffering from a tooth that had to be pulled, administered the gas to himself before the extraction. He felt no pain and proclaimed a new era in dentistry.

On January 10, 1845, Wells made an official demonstration of nitrous oxide as an anesthetic during surgery at the Massachusetts General Hospital in Boston. The demonstration proved to be a failure. The patient did not respond to the gas as expected and screamed in pain. Wells was laughed out of the hospital.

Lack of reliability was a problem with ether and chloroform, as well as nitrous oxide, in the years that these drugs were first being proposed for use as anesthetics. Sometimes they worked—they produced anesthesia—and sometimes they did not. Researchers today understand that one of the reasons for this unreliability was the absence of a strong set, or expectation of effect. Today expectation is so strong and well established that most people react to administration by becoming anesthetized. But even today there are patients who fail to respond to some anesthetics.

Although ether, chloroform, and nitrous oxide were widely used as recreational drugs for more than fifty years after the mid-nineteenth century, there is little evidence that this practice is indulged in today. Newspapers and magazines of the time featured lurid exposés of the abuse of these substances by college students, and many researchers extolled the "spiritual" qualities of the mental states created by these drugs. Much like LSD and mescaline today, nitrous oxide, ether, and chloroform were ecstatically held up as keys to hitherto-unavailable areas of human consciousness.

The next important laboratory discovery was the amphetamines that were first synthesized in 1887 in Germany. Although their stimulating effect on the central nervous system was noted, no practical applications for these interesting compounds were found for some forty years. In 1927, however, a number of practical uses for the drug were developed.

One of the first medicinal uses came in the treatment of alcoholics. It was found that amphetamines acted as effective sobering agents that overcame the effects of both narcotics and alcohol. Psychiatrists working in mental institutions with alcoholics obtained good results with Benzedrine, the trade name of the first commercially sold amphetamine.

In time more uses for this drug were found. It proved effective in the treatment of certain mild nervous depressions and, to a lesser extent, the more severe depressions accompanying some forms of nervous disorder. Benzedrine was effective in the control and treatment of narcolepsy, a condition marked by an uncontrollable desire to sleep. It is also used in certain forms of Parkinson's disease as a relaxant to relieve muscular rigidity.

A paradoxical use of the drug was found in hyperactive children. The amphetamines, which are powerful stimulants, seem to act as depressants when administered to these children. It acts to quiet them down and helps the hyperactive child concentrate in school. Amphetamines are still used in this context today.

Benzedrine was also found to dull the appetite and thus found another application in weight reduction treatment. Finally, the vasoconstrictive action of the drug which is similar to that of adrenaline produces an effective decongestant action. In this case, the drug acts to shrink the nasal mucous membrane. For someone suffering from hay fever, asthma, head colds, or sinusitis, this action allows free breathing. Amphetamines were used widely in inhalers for relief of these symptoms until the drug was outlawed for this purpose in 1965.

Although amphetamines, first sold commercially as Benzedrine, were available since 1927, the first extensive use in Europe did not occur until the Spanish Civil War (1936–1939) when the drug was given to German paratroopers. Benzedrine proved so effective in combating fatigue and anxiety that it was soon issued to all the soldiers in that tragic conflict.

In America the early history of amphetamines was similar to that in Europe. Benzedrine was introduced to this country in 1932, but it did not come into wide use until World War II. Wars, with the enormous strains they place on combatants, have always been times of increased drug use and experimentation. During World War II American servicemen in all the military branches were issued Benzedrine tablets as a matter of course. The pills helped servicemen stand up to the strain of combat. They relieved fatigue, as well as anxiety, and in many cases the users discovered that a pill made the difference between collapse and the ability to function.

Nor was this use limited to servicemen and women. Civilians in all walks of life discovered the stimulant effects of "bennies." Factory workers, farmers, truck drivers, typists, everyone was pushing himself to his limit during that war, and all appear to have discovered the potency that resided in a tiny medicinal tablet.

Although the use of amphetamines mushroomed during World War II (1941–1945), no serious abuse problems were reported. During this conflict, drug companies had perfected a number of amphetamine-based compounds tailored to specific needs and uses. These were introduced as Dexedrine, Methedrine, Desbutal, Dexoxyn, Alentol, Benzaginyl, and dozens of other trade names.

After the war, amphetamines were available to all and were used for a variety of purposes. Students cramming for examinations, doctors, truck drivers, and others who had to remain alert for extended periods "popped" Benzedrine tablets. Other amphetamines were used in weight-control regimens; still others were used as nasal decongestants. The drug companies kept finding more and more uses for the compounds they produced, and amphetamine use spread steadily.

The amphetamines are synthetic stimulants that are similar in most of their pharmacological effects to cocaine—a natural drug that came down to us from the Indians of South America. The second great class of synthetic drugs, barbiturates, can be thought of as artificial alcohol. The history of barbiturates parallels that of the amphetamines in most respects.

Barbiturates were originally developed as a substitute for alcohol. Before the turn of the century, alcohol was the favored drug that physicians prescribed for such conditions as anxiety, tension, and insomnia. Taken in reasonable doses, alcohol does tend to reduce anxiety and tension while it promotes sleep. In the mid-1800's, however, alcohol became the focus of a worldwide campaign of repression. Alcohol abuse, of course, was a serious social problem in all the Western world. Church groups, moralists of all persuasions, and public health organizations combined to create an almost irresistible pressure against the use of alcohol in any form and context. Its use as a medicine came under particularly strong censure.

There were other chemicals available that were effective in the treatment of these same symptoms, but these had serious drawbacks. Bromide salts, as one example, were used to induce sleep and relaxation, but their use always ran the risk of bromide poisoning. Chloral hydrate, another effective sedative and hypnotic, has a taste and odor that many find objectionable, and some intolerable.

It was in this atmosphere that two German chemists developed a compound derived from barbituric acid which they called barbital that had pronounced sedative and relaxant properties. The compound was tested extensively on animals and human volunteers and was found both effective as a sedative and relaxant and safe for human use. The first barbiturate was introduced into general medical practice under the name Veronal. A second barbiturate compound, phenobarbital, was introduced in 1912 as Luminal.

Both products were prescribed by doctors as substitutes for medically used alcohol. They were used widely to help sleep and as relaxants. Although some 2,500 barbiturate compounds have since been synthesized, 50 of which have found medical uses, Veronal and Luminal are still being marketed.

There are three types of barbiturates in common use today: (1) long-acting (barbital, phenobarbital); (2) intermediate-acting (amobarbital, butabarbital); (3) short-acting (pentobarbital, secobarbital). A fourth type that is ultrashort-acting (thiopental, thiamylal) have been introduced most recently. These barbiturates, however, are almost never administered orally in the form of pills, but are used primarily as intravenous anesthetic agents.

This classification is determined by the rates at which the different barbiturates are eliminated from the body by the kidneys and liver. The different compounds also tend to have variable effects on the user. Long-lasting barbiturates generally take longer to act. They tend to move more slowly in the blood but generally produce more profound and prolonged sedation. The intermediate- and short-acting barbiturates are more quickly metabolized, although they trigger faster reactions.

Like alcohol and the narcotics, barbiturates act to depress the central nervous system. In small doses, they are effective in relieving tension and anxiety without causing excessive drowsiness. In larger doses, as the depressant action spreads through the central nervous system, the user becomes increasingly drowsy and lethargic until sleep ensues. Although barbiturate sedation appears to resemble natural sleep, there are clinical differences. Experiments have shown, for example, that the rate of eye movement while dreaming is much slower under barbiturates and breathing is not quite as deep as in ordinary sleep.

Although barbiturates were originally introduced as relaxants and as aids to sleep, many more clinical applications have been developed. Certain barbiturates have been demonstrated to be useful as anticonvulsants in epilepsy and other similar conditions. Others are used as anesthetics in minor surgery, and they remain indispensable in preoperative anesthetics, where they act to calm the anxieties of patients being prepared for surgery. Barbiturates are also necessary for the treatment of high blood pressure and peptic ulcers.

The drawbacks in the use of barbiturates are almost exactly the same as those of alcohol. They are addictive and highly intoxicating. The user develops a tolerance to the drug and must escalate the dosage. Abrupt withdrawal produces symptoms that are identical to those suffered by alcoholic withdrawal.

Because of this marked similarity to alcohol, barbiturate abuse was recognized comparatively early. After the introduction of barbiturates to general medical practice in 1903, the use grew steadily, if not spectacularly. Throughout the 1930's, for example, barbiturates were used as sleeping pills and could be bought without prescriptions in most states.

The first reports of barbiturate abuse came in the early 1940's, when newspapers and magazines featured articles exposing these practices. People had discovered that one could get roaring drunk on barbiturates and proceeded to act on this new knowledge. The exposés, which received wide attention, helped spread the word, and abuse of these drugs grew. At first, this use was limited to adults, but then it was noted that increasingly younger users were being reported.

Still, it was not until the fateful 1960's that barbiturate abuse assumed menacing proportions. This decade, as we have already seen, appears to have marked a major turning point in many aspects of American society. In no area, however, was the change as profound and as upsetting as it was in drug preference. A generation of Americans suddenly emerged with an attitude toward drugs that was completely different from that of their parents. This generation gap has been extended into the 1970's and continues as a volatile element in society.

Actually, this change is not too difficult to trace. As we have seen, World War II introduced millions of Americans to potent, mind-altering drugs. Benzedrine was used universally to keep awake, while barbiturates induced sleep. In the stress and strain that war imposed on society, both these effects were vital. A generation of Americans came to know the magic that resided in a tiny pill.

During that war the pharmacological companies perfected and developed a variety of mind-affecting drugs. Depressants and stimulants, hallucinogens and tranquilizers, hypnotics were combined in almost numberless mixtures. In sterile laboratories, scientists had discovered a reliable key to mood and mental well-being. Some of these drugs revolutionized the treatment of mental patients. Before their development, many patients who were doomed to spend entire lives under constraint were able to assume normal lives outside institutions.

With the coming of peace, the drug companies turned to the marketing of the marvelous new compounds their scientists had developed. At the same time, television, which had also been perfected during the war, was becoming the most effective advertising medium ever known. It was inevitable that the two should join forces.

These were the conditions that prevailed in the late 1940's, following World War II. First of all, there were people, millions of them, who had been introduced to powerful stimulants and depressants. History tells us that many—if not most—people possess an inborn penchant for mind-altering drugs. These same people, following in the wake of the war, produced a bumper crop of babies, who reached their teens and twenties in the late 1950's and early 1960's.

Combine these factors, and we have a most interesting situation. We have a bumper crop of babies whose parents are accustomed to "pop" a pill whenever they feel tired, out-of-sorts, too tense, or just need a lift. At the same time, we have drug companies with thousands of powerful new drugs waiting to find a market. And to complete the picture, there is television, emerging as the most effective selling medium ever devised.

The drug companies not only produce these very interesting new drugs, but actively pursue new business. From the time they begin to understand, children are bombarded with messages cleverly designed by our best professionals with the specific purpose of inducing people to use drugs. Television, of course, becomes the favored marketplace and children a prime target.

These children grew up in a world where magic potions could cure everything from obesity to fatigue. No need to be tired, homely, listless, tense, hyperactive, sleepless, dull, fat or skinny—swallow a pill and get FAST! FAST! FAST! relief. These same children also see their parents popping pills. Daddy comes home tired—a "bennie" will fix him up. Mother is nervous and irritable—Miltown will do the trick. In many households, mothers provided children with a small dose of barbiturate to help them sleep.

Such a child, born in 1946, entered college in 1964—just in time to participate in the great drug explosion that is now racking the country. Remember, he or she has grown up with a familiarity with drugs that is totally new. He has seen them advertised endlessly, and perhaps, more significantly he has grown up seeing his parents using a variety of little "magic" tablets to help ease their problems and help them through their days.

He has no fear and few inhibitions in regard to drugs. They are a familiar factor in his life to an extent that his parents cannot even conceive. If one "bennie" makes him feel good, why not take two . . . or three . . . or four! Why not indeed? How bad can they be if Mommy takes them too?

Unfortunately, some of these drugs are very bad—fully as dangerous and damaging as alcohol. Among the worst offenders are the amphetamines and barbiturates. Barbiturates, of course, can be considered synthetic alcohol and share most of the drawbacks of this most popular American drug. Although the barbiturates—especially the long-acting types—are not as toxic as alcohol, they can do physical damage to the body.

179

They affect the liver and the kidneys when ingested over a long period of time.

It is the amphetamines, however, that are most damaging. Although these drugs are medically necessary in many cases and are among the safest when used as directed by physicians, their effects tend to encourage abuse. A powerful stimulant, an amphetamine creates an illusion of immense energy and omnipotence in the user. If enough of the drug is ingested, the user loses all sense of inadequacy and failure. He or she feels that there is nothing he or she cannot do or accomplish.

Tolerance to this exuberant effect is quickly developed, and more of the drug is necessary to achieve the same state. Finally, the addicted user injects the amphetamine directly into the bloodstream to experience the "rush" that makes him feel temporarily like a superman.

Alas, however, there are side effects. One, of course, is in the suppression of appetite. This property, which is so useful in control of weight, becomes occasionally exaggerated to the extent that the user cannot swallow. On an extended "speed" binge, the addict neglects eating and sleeping and in his hyperexcited state expends enormous stores of energy. He also suffers psychotic episodes in which he experiences paranoid delusion. Such a "run," or amphetamine binge, may last for as long as a week, or until the user finally collapses after having expended his store of energy.

Of course, the amphetamines do not create energy, and the store that is spent during a "speed run" must be paid for somehow. The price is nervous and physical exhaustion, malnutrition, and the destruction of muscle tissue that severe malnutrition almost always entails, plus lingering paranoiac fears.

We have our first reports of the speed freak, or amphetamine abuser who injects the drug into his veins, in the early 1960's. The practice may have originated during the Korean War (1950–1953). Amphetamines were available to soldiers and in the illegal markets of Korea high-grade heroin was also plentiful and cheap. One way of "mainlining" amphetamines was to mix it with heroin and inject the combination. With pure amphetamines, the initial rush after injection is generally too strong to allow for any pleasure. In order to tone down this effect, a depressant—heroin in this case—was combined in the mixture. One drug acted to soften the effect of the other, and the combination, according to adepts, supposedly provided a superior high to that of either taken alone.

By the early 1960's the speed freak became a familiar figure in the youth-drug culture that was beginning to take shape at that time. In San Francisco and New York, wherever young people congregated, the amphetamines were gulped, swallowed, and injected.

At the time amphetamines were readily obtainable from drugstores and through prescriptions which doctors wrote freely. They were also inexpensive—the wholesale price for methamphetamine was 75 cents for a thousand 5-milligram tablets. Authorities, worried about the growing abuse of these stimulants, enforced the existing laws beginning in about 1962. Parallel to this development came both the smuggling and diverting of legitimate sources to the black market and the emergence of clandestine laboratories that produced the drugs in quantity. As a result of police suppression, the prices of amphetamines rose dramatically, making a very profitable operation out of both smuggling and manufacturing illegal amphetamines.

Although speed rarely kills, and the psychotic delusions that ingestion of the drug precipitates are almost never permanent, the short-range effects of amphetamine abuse is often disastrous. Like no other drug, with the exception perhaps of alcohol, the amphetamines tend to dominate all aspects of the user's life. When on a run, the speed freak neglects everything and becomes totally absorbed in his mania. Although most users are aware that the paranoid delusions they experience stem from the effects of the drug, they still react to them and can become aggressive and violent.

Today, fortunately, the speed freak appears to be a dwindling category on the drug scene. Apparently, addicts are not necessarily bent on self-destruction. Many people, seeing the effects of amphetamine injection on heavy users, tend to steer away from such an experience. Although "speed does not kill," it does leave the user wrung out and helpless. Pragmatic experience, in this case, appears to be putting a brake on a dangerous drug abuse.

In this context, the myths and half-truths that surround drugs are one of the principal reasons for the spread of such dangerous practices. In the early 1960's all drugs were lumped together as equally dangerous and immoral. Marijuana and LSD were picked out for particular censure. Teen-agers in high schools and colleges were bombarded with lectures, films, and pamphlets warning them that LSD and "pot" were deadly and addictive. When they tried them and discovered that the scare stories were not true, the youngsters interpreted this to mean that all the stories about drugs were Establishment lies.

Barbiturate abuse, however, continues to grow and is recognized as one of our most serious drug problems today. Yet even if all barbiturates and amphetamines were eliminated, the problem would not be solved. In laboratories all over the world, scientists work to find new compounds that affect mood and well-being. New drugs appear daily, and their marketing and distribution remain one of the nation's largest industries.

As soon as one drug is taken off the market as being addictive or otherwise dangerous, two more appear to take its place. Presently, the new drug "menace" is Quaalude—methaqualone, sold as Quaalude, Sopor, and other trade names. This is a nonbarbiturate tranquilizer that has been marketed as a relaxant and aid to sleep.

Over the past year, however, methaqualone has grown in popularity as a street drug, particularly among high school and college students. Users report that its mild, sedative action leaves a mellow sensation and that the drug heightens sexual satisfaction.

Although the tranquilizer was promoted as a safe, nonaddictive aid, physicians involved in drug treatment have found that methaqualone is addicting. Indeed, they claim that the addiction is harder to control than the heroin habit. Dangerous side effects from large doses that include delirium, coma, and internal bleeding have been reported. Methaqualone now comes under the same regulations as such other addictive prescription drugs as morphine, methadone, and amphetamines.

The laboratory has become the principal supplier of drugs. Chemists and pharmacologists are synthesizing an almost infinite variety of mind-altering drugs. Some of these are more potent than anything in common use today, and some have bizarre effects that far surpass the drugs we know. Many of these drugs will reach the market as aids in sleep and relaxation, as stimulants and depressants. Many, like methaqualone, will eventually be found to be addicting.

These drug companies must sell their products in order to exist, and to do so, they must promote them as best they possibly can. Today drug companies spend literally hundreds of millions of dollars to convince people to purchase their wares. In 1972, according to testimony by Senator Mike Gravel of Alaska, some 225,000,000 prescriptions for psychotropic drugs were issued.

Too many of these, Senator Gravel contends, came about only as a result of the enormous advertising campaigns conducted by drug companies in medical journals. In these advertisements, aimed at the physician, doctors are urged to prescribe psychotropics for almost any imaginable ailment, anxiety, or depression. One such advertisement, cited by the Senator, a three-page, gaudily illustrated spread for Ritalin, a stimulant manufactured by CIBA, discovered an entirely new mental ailment that this drug could cure: *environmental depression.* Tensions generated by our environment, the advertisement goes on to say, that include traffic jams, electric failures, noise, smog, and other pollutants, may be expressed as "listlessness, fatigue, or vague symptoms of depression."

Although the advertisements do not claim a cure—"Ritalin will not help all depressed patients faced with environmental problems, and it certainly won't change those problems or an individual's response to them. But Ritalin can improve outlook and help get your patients moving again"—they do promise help.

In our confusing world where drugs are promoted as boons to mankind or as unmitigated evils that are threatening to destroy us, a practical solution appears nonexistent. Any realistic appraisal of the situation must conclude that all attempts to stop people from using mood-altering drugs are doomed to fail. The problem is that we have mixed up morality with what should be a medical question.

We have deemed the taking of certain drugs to be immoral

and evil in itself and have tried to enforce these notions of morality through police power and repressive laws. If, according to Dr. Joel Fort, a recognized authority on drugs: "we had been committed to actually solving the problem more than to whipping the people who have it, we could have been seriously and creatively looking for real solutions . . . instead we have tried to beat one another into submission. . . "

9. WHY?

THE desire to alter one's mood or state of consciousness appears to be inborn in the human species. Perhaps it would be more accurate to speak of need rather than desire. Man has always exhibited this compulsion to get beyond his own skin periodically by whatever means possible. Meditation, fasting, chants, exercises, torture, orgies, music, dance—all have been and are used to achieve this end. Drugs in their mysterious interaction with the human psyche provide the quickest and easiest means for altering consciousness.

There is evidence indicating that this desire to alter consciousness goes beyond man. Many animals are attracted by drugs. The craving that cats exhibit for catnip and cattle for locoweed and the manner in which these creatures react to these plants are examples of drug compulsion. Squirrels react similarly to certain pine-cone seeds, and bees and wasps apparently get drunk on fermented sap whenever the opportunity arises—neglecting their regular duties while under the influence. These are the most familiar examples of drug use among animals. There are more. Animals appear to have a similar need to alter consciousness that humans exhibit.

One species produces a drug in its body that is utilized in a unique system of self-defense. The yellow rat snake, a common reptile found throughout southeastern America, exudes a chemical when attacked by bobcats much as a skunk exudes scent. The snake's discharge, however, appears to alter the state of consciousness of the attacking cat. It acts in seconds to transform an aggressive killer into an affectionate playmate.

Under influence of this discharge, the cat stops its attack and fondles the snake. It rubs against it sensually, rolling over on its back in an unseemly display of goodwill. Finally, the snake is released and goes on its way none the worse for having been party to this strange encounter. The life of the snake was spared because it exuded a chemical which altered the state of consciousness of the attacking cat. The predator sacrifices a meal for the pleasure of the high afforded by what can only be a drug given off by the yellow rat snake.

In laboratories, researchers are studying strains of rats and mice that have been addicted to morphine, heroin, and other drugs for generations. These addicted rodents display a compulsion for their drug that is similar in most respects to that experienced by their human counterparts. The craving they exhibit appears stronger than the supposedly dominant instincts for food and sex. Addicted mice and rats will regularly pass up opportunities to satisfy both needs in favor of their desire for drugs. They also reveal a readily recognized withdrawal syndrome when administration of the drug is interrupted. Withdrawal syndrome includes restlessness, pugnacity, and a characteristic bodily reaction called "wet-dog shakes" because of the resemblance to a dog shaking water off its back.

The desire for drugs is not restricted to the human species. It extends across the animal kingdom. We should not be surprised, therefore, that our society includes many people who exhibit a need for drugs. Most societies, however, do not have the kind of drug problem with which we have to contend. But then few other societies have handled this very human need so ineptly.

Drugs appear to be a part of life and living. They may be as necessary as food and shelter. Indeed, it would be as difficult to imagine a society without some kind of drug as it would be without some form of religion. Alcohol, tobacco, and opium, all highly addictive drugs, have played important and even dominant roles in the economic and social history of the United States just as they have in other countries all over the world.

Because of their ability to alter mood or state of consciousness, drugs have always been eagerly sought after. The great problem stems from the fact that those substances that alter mood are generally addicting. Once the user becomes addicted, he finds it all but impossible to stop. His body demands the presence of the addictive substance. He finds that he cannot function normally without constant administration of the drug.

There is no effective cure for addiction and no reliable method for stopping the condition once it is established as far as we are able to determine. Those few people who manage to control their addiction—who stop smoking, successfully give up alcohol, or "kick" the heroin habit—are rare. Some authorities argue that the ability to withdraw from a drug, any drug, merely demonstrates the fact that the subject was not truly addicted in the first place!

Although neither the physiological nor psychological basis

of drug addiction is understood, we do know that the compulsion of the addict is one of the most powerful cravings known to man. The addict is generally helpless in the face of what he experiences as an irresistible need.

This need is a fundamental factor in drug addiction, and it appears to have been ignored by those people who formulated our drug laws and those who administer them. These laws and the public attitude toward drug addiction which makes the laws possible are based on the mistaken assumption that the addict can stop taking drugs if only he or she really wanted to. The answer to the problem of addiction in this popular view is simply a matter of exerting one's willpower or, that having failed, embarking on a *course of treatment* that will effect a cure!

To see how mistaken such an assumption is one need only visit a hospital ward where lung cancer is being treated. Although the causal role of cigarette smoking in lung cancer has been thoroughly established, it is not unusual to see patients smoking as they are wheeled to the operating theater. There is no question that these people *want* to stop smoking. They cannot—though their lives depend on it!

Those rare individuals who manage to stop smoking, drinking, or "shooting" heroin actually exacerbate the problem. They offer a tantalizing promise that cannot be fulfilled in the overwhelming majority of cases. Statistics show that the rate of recidivism is more than 90 percent in all addiction.

Two studies of recidivism rates among patients discharged from the narcotics hospital in Lexington, Kentucky, showed that within four years the rate was 97 percent in one study and 93.4 percent in the second study. The first study involved 453 Lexington dischargees and the second involved 1,912 ex-patients.

In California, Dr. John C. Kramer and Richard A. Bass

conducted a study of more than 8,000 addicts committed to the California Rehabilitation Center for Addicts. Out of this number 300, or about 4 percent, were considered successfully detoxified. And even this figure is unreliable according to the Kramer-Bass findings because a sizable portion of these successful cases may never have been addicted.

Professor William A. Hunt, psychologist at Loyola University in Chicago, and Dr. Joseph D. Matarazzo, of the Department of Medical Psychology, University of Oregon School of Medicine, reviewed the relapse rate among attenders of seventeen antismoking clinics that kept valid and reliable figures on follow-up studies of the people involved. The combined relapse rate of those who successfully stopped smoking reached 83 percent in forty-eight months and approached 90 percent in sixty months. These, of course, were highly motivated people who had voluntarily entered the clinics.

Still, the problem racking the nation is not addiction in itself. We are accustomed to living with tens of millions of addicts in all walks of life. Cigarette smokers are taken in stride, although most are so heavily addicted that they must have a "fix" at least once every waking hour of their lives. Despite the enormous cost in lives, health, and money, no social disapprobation is attached to cigarette addicts. The same holds true for drinkers. We tolerate millions of alcoholics and even more near alcoholics and often look on and treat them rather affectionately. Few of us consider them monsters.

The problem that generates most of the turmoil is specific. It is involved almost exclusively with heroin. This is the ultimate, the hardest of the "hard drugs," the mere mention of which causes decent people to shudder in disgust. Let us, therefore, examine this worst of all drugs in more detail. One might justifiably suspect that there was something particularly hideous in the physical or mental effects of heroin to cause such a panic. Yet examination of its effects reveals little, outside of its addicting quality, to explain this notoriety.

Indeed, if we were to approach drugs from a purely pharmacological viewpoint, a good case could be made for heroin in comparison with most other drugs. As far as we know, heroin is not toxic unless administered in massive doses; it does no damage to the body or its organs; it has no negative effects on brain function in the sense that it can cause insanity or mental impairment; it is not intoxicating and does not cause the user to lose control of mental or bodily functions; there is no evidence that heroin, of itself, compels the user to crime. It is also relatively inexpensive. *The five grains or so a day that would amply supply most addicts could be bought for five or six cents in a legal market.*

We know that the heroin addict who can afford to maintain his habit without depriving himself of food and other necessities cannot be recognized as such through either physical appearance or overt actions. Elaborate chemical tests of urine and blood samples must be made in order to identify him. Those who can satisfy their cravings without resort to crime can live indefinitely without being detected. Certainly, it would be impossible for an alcoholic to hide his condition the same way. The physical effects of his drug are too obvious to hide.

If this is so, what is all the fuss about? If it is possible for an addict to satisfy his need for heroin for ten years, as an addict testified on a program televised over WNET recently, without his employers, co-workers, friends, or even family suspecting his addiction, how heinous can the condition be? Why all the outrage?

Why, indeed! In this common attitude we find the most fascinating question posed by the addiction problem. Why has this deviant behavior been singled out for so much horror and detestation? Why is heroin addiction considered to be so degrading and dehumanizing?

These are difficult questions to answer. The arguments most commonly advanced against heroin addiction cannot account for the public attitude. One of the principal reasons for condemning this habit, for example, is the evidence indicating that heroin kills. This allegation is true, but only in a manner of speaking. Heroin addicts die. Some 2,500 died in 1973 as a result of the illegal use of this drug.

It can be demonstrated, however, that most of these deaths were not caused by any effect of heroin itself on the body. They were the results primarily of conditions that stem from the illegal status of the drug. The largest number of heroin-connected deaths were caused by infections and diseases passed on through the use of unsterile hypodermic equipment, followed by deaths owing to malnutrition and exposure that are a consequence of the exorbitant price of black-market heroin. Next in line come deaths caused by poisonous adulterants in street-bought drugs.

Some deaths are believed to be caused by a fatal and dramatic reaction to the combination of alcohol or barbiturates with heroin. This combination causes a readily identified reaction that includes almost immediate death from breathing failure owing to lung congestion. Although the cause of this syndrome is not completely understood, those deaths attributed to it are generally listed as OD's (overdose deaths). Relatively few deaths are actually caused by heroin overdose.

When we compare the deaths attributed to heroin in America, for whatever reasons, with the toll from tobacco and alcohol, this objection makes no sense at all. In 1973 fewer than 3,000 deaths were traced to heroin. During the same year about 250,000 deaths were attributed to tobacco—80,000 from lung cancer, 35,000 from emphysema, about 125,000 from heart and circulatory ailments, and the remainder from a variety of rarer tobacco-induced diseases and conditions. Alcohol killed about 350,000 people in the same year according to figures of the Surgeon General's office. Obviously, it is not the deaths attributed to heroin addiction that we object to so strongly.

Another argument commonly advanced against heroin addiction is the objection of being enslaved by a drug. The addict, it is pointed out, is compelled by powerful physical and psychological compulsions to constant use of the drug. He has become a slave to addiction. Certainly, this is a valid objection, and no one can deny the compulsive, enslaving nature of heroin addiction. But there are tens of millions of addicts in our midst all the time, and no one seems to object to them very seriously. The smoker and the alcoholic are as enslaved to a drug as the heroin addict. Again, it cannot be addiction in itself that is so objectionable.

Finally, heroin is condemned because of the crime associated with the drug. This allegation, once more, is true. Heroin addicts steal, prostitute themselves, embezzle, shoplift, break into homes, become pushers, and commit any number of other crimes to obtain the money necessary to support a very expensive habit. None of these crimes, however, can be traced to any intrinsic effect of the drug itself on the addict. Indeed, there is evidence that heroin addiction tends to subdue rage and may be a deterrent to the more violent crimes.

The crime associated with heroin addiction is almost all the result of the price gouging practiced by dealers. The five grains or so a day the addict needs in order to function costs $50 and more on today's black market—an expense few legitimate incomes can support. Addict crime—outside of that stemming from the fact that an addict is a criminal just by being—is involved almost exclusively in raising money to pay for illegal drugs.

Recent studies indicate that the volume of crime attributed to drug addicts is exaggerated. These findings suggest that if all addicts were to disappear tomorrow, the crime rate would fall, but not as dramatically as many of us might think. Crime rates are rising all over the world, even in areas without any drug problem, and drugs do not appear to be the dominant factor in this increase.

One such study was directed by Dr. William C. Eckerman, of the Research Triangle Institute, for the Bureau of Narcotics and Dangerous Drugs in 1970–1971. His findings are very revealing. The study was carried out by personal interviews and urine analysis of 1,899 people arrested in Chicago, Los Angeles, New Orleans, Brooklyn, San Antonio, and St. Louis.

The results showed clearly that in the major categories of violent crime—criminal homicide, forcible rape, aggravated assault—nondrug users were substantially more often charged than drug users. It was found that the drug user was primarily involved in "acquisitive" crime rather than "violent" crime. Thus 17.1 percent of all drug users in the study had been charged with robbery; another 20.6 percent were charged with burglary; 4.8 percent were charged with auto theft; and the remainder were charged with violations of the narcotics laws.

Dr. Eckerman's study also suggested that drug addicts—as reflected in arrest records—numbered no more than 35 percent of the convicted prison population on an average. If these figures reflect crime statistics at all, they indicate that although addicts are responsible for a considerable portion of the nation's crime, they are not the major factor in this incidence.

When we attempt to find a rational basis for the hysteria attached to heroin addiction, it is impossible to isolate those factors inherent in the effects of the drug itself that are responsible. In order to explain this abhorrence, we must look to more obscure psychological areas of human experience. In short, our attitudes are irrational!

An example of this irrationality on a grand scale was provided by former New York State Governor Nelson Rockefeller in his annual State of the State address to the legislature in Albany on January 18, 1973. In this speech, the governor proposed sweeping antidrug legislation that included *mandatory life sentences* for drug pushers and addicts convicted of violent crimes without exception and with no provision allowed for plea bargaining.

The governor argued that New York State had tried everything to stem the growing tide of addiction without success. The programs designed to cure addiction and to rehabilitate addicts, which cost the people of New York more than $1 billion, were most notable for their failure. They neither cured addiction nor stemmed its growth. None of the programs, the governor pointed out, could show any figures that might so much as encourage continuation, let alone warrant it. Since treatment failed, incarceration for life was the solution offered by Governor Rockefeller.

When Governor Rockefeller made his State of the State speech before the New York legislature in Albany, his proposals for these draconian antidrug measures evoked stronger and more enthusiastic applause than any other made in the address. *Lock them up and throw the keys away* is what the governor proposed and the state lawmakers cheered. Worse yet, they passed a slightly modified version of the bill!

Why this lust for punishment and revenge? Why this cry, if not for the blood, then for the lives of addicts and pushers?

Certainly, one of the most important factors is the misinformation that envelops the entire question of drug addiction. In their zeal to condemn, reformists have created a picture of drugs and addiction that has little or no connection with reality. The addict has been depicted as an unspeakable ogre and monster so often that few of us could recognize a real addict if we saw one. This barrage of deliberate distortion affects all our thinking. It has created an atmosphere that made it possible for the prosecuting attorney (*State of California v. Robinson,* 1962) to introduce this florid speech into a court of law:

> To be a confirmed drug addict is to be one of the walking dead. . . . The teeth have rotted out, the appetite is lost, and the stomach and intestines do not function properly. The gall bladder becomes inflamed; eyes and skin turn a bilious yellow; in some cases membranes turn a flaming red; the partition separating the nostrils is eaten away . . . breathing is difficult. . . . Boils and abscesses plague the skin; gnawing pain wracks the body. Nerves snap; vicious twitching develops. Imaginary fantastic fears blight the mind and sometimes complete insanity results. . . . Such is the torment of being a drug addict; such is the plague of being one of the walking dead.

Walking dead? It makes for colorful reading, and we can be certain that the jury in the case was properly impressed. More significant, however, is the fact that most people in America would probably agree that this was an accurate depiction of heroin addiction and its effects on the body.

Alas, nothing in this description is true! Heroin does not rot the teeth, has no effect on the gallbladder, does not turn membranes a flaming red, will not eat away the partition between the nostrils (where did this idea come from?); nor will it turn the skin or eyes a bilious or any other shade of yellow. The fact that this description was accepted in a court of law without challenge testifies to the depth of the misconception surrounding drug addiction.

This kind of distortion alone, however, no matter how pervasive, is still not enough to explain the intensity of our attitudes. Americans, after all, are accustomed to dealing with lies, misinformation, and distortions on an even more massive scale. We take the exaggerations and hyperbole of politicians and advertisers in stride without too much notice. We watch "real-life" dramas on movie and television screens that are as far removed from life and living as imagination permits and are not greatly affected. Why should we be so gullible when it comes to drug addiction?

One of the reasons may be sexual in nature. Despite all the talk about permissiveness and revolution, we are still a repressed, sin-haunted society. There could be a symbolism in the act of injecting one's self, a self-violation, an analogy to intercourse that we cannot cope with rationally. This fear is in our language. "Go fuck yourself" is the worst thing one person can say to another, and this—symbolically—is precisely what the addict is doing.

Worse yet is the belief that the addict is experiencing a secret, unspeakable pleasure. A pleasure, moreover, that is denied ordinarily prudent, clean-living, cigarette-smoking, alcohol-swilling citizens. The addict haunts straight society with dreams of possible pleasures missed, pleasures most of us are too timid to savor for ourselves. This we cannot forgive!

There is one more element that could play a role in our irrational attitudes. All societies appear to have a need for a scapegoat, for a deviant group that becomes the focal point for the ills from which that society suffers. In Nazi Germany this need was cynically manipulated by a corrupt leadership who created a scapegoat in the form of the "alien Jew."

In an unprecedented propaganda campaign, Jews were singled out for vicious attack. They were depicted as the defilers, the despoilers who degraded a noble Aryan people and culture. All the ills with which Germany was saddled at the time were blamed upon the Jews. It was the Jew who was responsible for unemployment, a disastrous inflation, and the hunger of the masses of poor German working people. The Jews were behind the corruption, the immorality, the licentious permissiveness that plagued Germany.

This delegation of the Jew as scapegoat was accepted by the majority of the German people—or at least it was not opposed. It was a convenient foil for the real frustration and loss experienced by the Germans. The country had serious social and economic problems following defeat in World War I. How much easier was it to blame the Jews than to deal with the problems realistically?

The drug addict in America occupies a position in society that is similar in many respects to that of the Jews in Nazi Germany. Even the choice of language used in the propaganda is similar in both cases. In Germany, the Jew was depicted as the defiler and despoiler of the pure Aryan people, as the corrupter of youth and authority, as the wellspring of all evil.

How many times have we heard addicts described in

frighteningly similar terms? We also look on the addict as defiler and despoiler of good, clean American youth, as the corrupter of authority and source of evil. Crime in the streets? It's the addicts! Unrest in the cities? Blame the junkies! Poverty and dirt? What can you expect with so many heroin freaks running loose!

The solution?

Lock them up and throw the keys away!

Somehow, the solution also sounds familiar.

Drug addiction is an emotion-packed issue. It touches on shadowy, vague areas of the human psyche. It stirs up ancient fears and releases vast reservoirs of hostility. At best, it is a most difficult question to deal with rationally. At worst, it encourages a lynch-mob mentality that feeds on itself. In one way or another, all of us are affected by what appears to be an unsolvable problem.

Because it is so emotional an issue, it is imperative that those who assume responsibility in this area do so as rationally and unemotionally as possible. It is one thing for a layman to believe that drug addiction is the most horrible degradation a human can lower himself to, another for a governor to propose that addicts be locked away forever.

For an ambitious politician, of course, such a proposal makes sense. It will find favor among the vast number of misinformed, manipulated people with an irrational bias against addiction. The governor can boast to them of his "toughness" and "hard head" as though they were virtues. But as a governor who has access to all the pertinent information Mr. Rockefeller must also have been aware that his draconian measures will do nothing to solve a most serious problem. On the contrary, they can only aggravate an already-critical situation. In its adverse effects on society, Mr. Rockefeller's cynicism is more damaging than that of the worst pusher or dealer.

We know little about addiction in a pharmacological sense. No one can say for certain how addiction is established and why the condition is maintained. We do not know how the addicting molecules interact with the body to produce their effects. We do know, however, a good deal about the enforcement of antidrug laws. In this area we have considerable experience to fall back upon.

Fifty-three years ago the government of the United States outlawed alcohol. The law of the land made the sale, possession, and transport of alcoholic beverages a high crime. This law remained in effect for fifteen years. The result was disaster. From its inception the law was flouted. It did succeed, however, in making criminals out of tens of millions of Americans. It brought an underworld crime empire into existence that exerts a maleficent influence on society to this day. It established a tradition of corruption on all levels of authority that undermined respect for our laws and lawmakers. Even more important, it failed! Prohibition did not stop people from drinking alcohol. When the law was finally repealed, an entire nation breathed a sigh of relief.

Attempts to banish marijuana have been equally efficacious. When federal antimarijuana laws were first passed in 1937, an estimated 100,000 people had used the drug in the United States. There was no marijuana problem, and most Americans never even heard of the drug.

Today, after having been illegal for thirty-seven years and the subject of an intense suppressive effort by both local police and federal agents, marijuana is smoked by millions of Americans, and its use is growing steadily. It has reached the point where enforcement officials concede that it can no longer be stopped. Marijuana is apparently here to stay. The futility of the antimarijuana laws makes their continued existence an embarrassment.

Cigarettes had a very similar history. During the first two decades of this century, when cigarettes were beginning to be manufactured and sold in quantity, most states passed laws prohibiting or restricting sales of this commodity. Minors, along with women, who often fell into the same legal category, were forbidden to smoke. Sales to either was a criminal offense.

In 1921 fourteen states passed cigarette prohibition laws and twenty-eight additional states had enacted various anticigarette legislation. In Florida, for example, it was illegal for anyone under the age of twenty-one to smoke cigarettes, and such an offense was punishable by fine or jail sentence. In Kansas, Georgia, West Virginia, and Nebraska, sale of cigarettes to minors and women was prohibited. In Maine an offer to sell cigarettes to minors was a crime, and in Pennsylvania a minor who refused to divulge the source of cigarettes could be fined, imprisoned, or certified to the juvenile courts. Most of these laws are still in effect.

The result: Cigarette smoking grew steadily from year to year until today 50,000,000 to 60,000,000 Americans indulge this dangerous practice. In 1973 tobacco companies celebrated their best year in history—for the first time, sales of cigarettes exceeded the 600 billion mark!

Experience, painfully acquired, has demonstrated time and again the futility of outlawing drugs. Making a drug illegal is the worst possible way of dealing with a drug problem. We know that this step, in and of itself, guarantees a progression of evils compounded from the original condition the law was meant to alleviate.

Worms, rats, monkeys, infants, all learn from their mistakes. Once burned, the baby automatically withdraws its hand from a flame. And even a worm will learn to avoid painful obstacles in its path. Society, unhappily, does not appear to possess this same learning ability. If we do not learn from our mistakes, we are doomed to repeat them. How many times?

Any attempt to deal realistically with the drug problem must take two factors into account: (1) No society, as far as we know, has succeeded in eliminating addicting drugs or addicts; (2) the addict is compelled by what may be the most powerful craving experienced by man, and this condition, in 90 percent of all cases, can be neither cured nor alleviated.

To ignore these facts is to invite failure. Yet our national approach would seem to avoid them deliberately. We speak glibly of treatment centers where addicts can go for a *cure*, as though addiction were like pneumonia or measles. Our government, in its effort to *protect its citizens*, has gone so far as to buy up the opium crop of an entire nation in a vain attempt to stop drugs *arbitrarily deemed illegal* from reaching our shores.

In these ill-conceived attempts, our society seems to have blundered into a situation that cannot conceivably be made worse. We have lived up to Murphy's Law with a vengeance: Everything we could possibly do wrong we have done wrong!

Look at the situation we are in today. We have made heroin illegal. This, of course, does not deter the addict. If anything, it makes him more determined. Legal or no, he must have his supply. Since legitimate sources are denied him, the addict is left to the tender mercies of gangster smugglers who operate without legal restraint or control.

This criminal element supplies the drug at a price—the absolute maximum the traffic will bear, which turns out to be about $50 for five grains of questionable quality in the case of heroin. This price, according to recent police estimates, may have risen to $75 to $100 in New York State. This, of course, will be a direct result of Governor Rockefeller's new law. Increased risk means increased price.

This price structure ensures a continuous supply of the drug because the traffic is so profitable. It also guarantees corruption of enforcement agency personnel. In a situation where $25 worth of a product can be sold for an eventual $200,000, there is more than enough money available to assure wholesale police corruption.

The price also compels the addict into crime. Not many legitimate incomes can afford to maintain a $50 daily expense. In order to meet this price, the addict steals, breaks into homes, shoplifts, and does whatever else is necessary to raise the money to pay for his drug. The predictable result: crime and alienation of the public that eventually pays for addiction.

At the same time, the media, in their effort to entertain a mass audience rather than inform, have presented a picture of heroin addiction that is at once frightening, ghastly, and tempting. If the eating of yogurt were suddenly outlawed and the act were depicted as the ultimate in human degradation, several hundred thousand people in America who never dreamed of eating yogurt would rush to sample this new forbidden fruit.

This irresponsible and sensational publicity guarantees a continuous supply of addicts while turning the public against them. The addict is thus isolated from society and is forced into a distinctive subculture with its own drug-oriented mores, rules, and morality. To complete the picture, public opinion makes it all but impossible for the addict to reenter society even in the rare instances where he or she manages to kick the habit.

Not an encouraging picture. Can we think of any way to make the situation bleaker? It does not seem likely. Still, it is even more difficult to formulate an acceptable solution. The situation is so rigid and complex that one is tempted to give up in despair. What do we really want? Even so simple a question is almost impossible to answer.

Do we want to eliminate all mind-affecting drugs? To be consistent, this would have to be our goal. It makes little sense to outlaw one category of drugs and permit another to be used openly—especially when the legal drugs are every bit as damaging as the illegal ones.

Perhaps this should be our goal—the elimination of all mind-altering drugs from American life. This would mean that along with narcotics, hallucinogens, amphetamines, barbiturates, marijuana, cocaine, and other so-called hard drugs, we would have to abolish alcohol and tobacco. The latter are just as addicting and are even more damaging in a physiological sense than the illegal drugs.

We can advance convincing arguments for even so drastic a step. All drugs are potentially dangerous. All, when used to excess, will cause damage. Ideally, all drugs should be avoided since none are necessary for life—but then, neither is music.

Man does not live by bread alone, and history indicates that the goal of a drug-free society is impractical. As far as we know, drugs cannot be eliminated from society. Whenever and wherever such a course of action has been attempted, the result has inevitably been disastrous. Drugs, like death and taxes, will always be with us.

If we cannot eliminate drugs from society, the next best thing might be to make their presence cause as little damage and disruption as possible. We know of societies in which drugs played dominant religious and social roles without ever becoming disruptive or damaging. The American Indians used powerful drugs without developing a "drug problem." Perhaps we can learn from them./

Actually, we need not go so far afield. Sixty-one years ago (1913) anyone could walk into any pharmacy in America and purchase, at reasonable cost, all the heroin, morphine, hashish, cocaine, or any other drug his heart desired (ether was a favorite at the time). The year 1913 is not notorious for either licentiousness or crime. Indeed, the per capita rate for crime was about a tenth of what it is today. Older people still speak nostalgically about those "good old days" when it was safe to walk down the streets and nobody needed locks on their doors. In Central Park sheep ran loose on the Sheep Meadow, and no one would think of defacing a national monument.

True, the per capita rate of addiction was considerably higher than it is today, but this rate did not disrupt society. There was no "drug problem" as we know it today. Those people who needed drugs simply bought them at the corner drugstore. They were not looked on as ogres by the rest of society, nor did exorbitant prices force them into crime. Here, again, we could profit from the experience of the past.

As a first step we might begin by telling the truth about drugs. The blanket of lies and distortions that envelop the question is one of its most damaging aspects. We should put a stop to the sensational stories and the hysterical, tantalizing presentation that is the most common treatment in newspapers and television. The best thing, perhaps, might be simply to ignore the question and not to publicize it at all.

Certainly, the mass of misinformation does nothing to help the problem. It does not act as a deterrent and can do real damage. Should a teen-ager, as one example, smoke a marijuana cigarette expecting some kind of overwhelming experience and discover that he feels nothing, he will forever after suspect whatever the authorities tell him about any drug.

We should know what drugs do and do not do. We should be made aware that tobacco and alcohol contain drugs that are as addictive and as dangerous as heroin in every sense but the legal one. Even more important, we should know about the nature of addiction in all its aspects. We should be made aware that addiction—whether it be to coffee, tobacco, alcohol, or heroin—is a permanent condition once established, and there is no treatment that will cure the addict.

Another step which would be immediately beneficial would be getting the government—on federal, state, and local levels—out of the drug business. In one aspect at least, Governor Rockefeller was right. None of the heralded addiction treatment and prevention programs have worked. Let us put a stop to them—to the Halfway Houses, the Synanons, the Phoenix programs, and all the other money-wasting, unrealistic efforts to stop and *cure* addiction. Such a step would save some $600,000,000 of the taxpayers' money every year, a benefit not to be sneered at in this period of history.

Finally, heroin and all other drugs should be made legally available. Great Britain, with a smaller, more homogeneous society, but one comparable to our own, does make drugs legally available. It has been notably free of drug-related crime and indeed has a considerably lower addiction rate than ours. Legalization would reduce the cost to the addict drastically and would drive the gangsters out of the drug business since there could be no profit in it for them. It would do away with most addict-related crimes since junkies would no longer have to steal in order to obtain their drugs. It would also eliminate the enormous cost of maintaining narcotic squads and expensive antismuggling operations. We might get more addicts this way, and we might not. We do not know. And even if we did, what difference would it make if their presence did not disrupt society?

Dr. Andrew Weil, author of *The Natural Mind,* a study of drugs and their effects, who has done a great deal of research and objective thinking about drugs, has this to say about heroin, the worst of all drugs: "If heroin could be isolated from its context in our society, we would soon see that the drug per se is relatively innocuous. . . ."

We might discover that what Dr. Weil says is true and the problem would disappear. Remember, the drinking of coffee was considered so depraved and immoral in sixteenth-century Spain that the possession of a single coffee bean was punishable by death!

BIBLIOGRAPHY

ABSE, D., *Medicine on Trial*. New York, Crown Press, 1969.

ALPERT, RICHARD, PhD; COHEN, SIDNEY, MD; and SCHILLER, LAWRENCE, *LSD*. New York, New American Library, 1966.

ANSLINGER, HARRY J., and OURSLER, FULTON, *The Murderers*. New York, Farrar, Straus & Cudahy, 1961.

AUSABEL, DAVID P., *Drug Addiction: Physiological and Social Aspects*. New York, Random House, 1958.

BAUDELAIRE, CHARLES, *Les Paradis Artificiels*, trans. by Norman Cameron. London, Weidenfeld & Nicolson Ltd., 1860.

BECKER, HOWARD S., *Outsiders: Studies in the Sociology of Deviance*, New York, The Free Press, 1963.

BLOOMQUIST, E. R., *Marijuana*. Beverly Hills, Calif., Glencoe Press, 1968.

BLUM, DR. RICHARD H., and Associates, *Students and Drugs*, The Jossey-Bass Behavioral Science Series. Berkeley, Calif., Stamford University Press, 1969.

——, *Utopiates: The Use and Users of LSD-25*. New York, Atherton Press, 1964.

BROOKS, JEROME, *The Mighty Leaf.* Boston, Little, Brown and Company, 1952.

BROTMAN, RICHARD, and FREEMAN, ALFRED, *A Community Mental Health Approach to Drug Addiction,* Washington, D.C., U.S. Dept. of Health, Education and Welfare, 1966.

BURROUGHS, WILLIAM, *Naked Lunch.* New York, Grove Press, 1959.

CASHMAN, JOHN, *The LSD Story.* Greenwich, Conn., Fawcett Publications, 1966.

CHEIN, ISIDOR, et al., *The Road to H: Narcotics, Delinquency and Social Policy.* New York, Basic Books, Inc., 1964.

COHEN, SIDNEY, MD, *The Drug Dilemma.* New York, McGraw-Hill, 1969.

COLES, A., *The Grass Pipe.* Boston, Atlantic Monthly Press, 1969.

COOK, JAMES GRAHAM, *Drug-Laws and Legislation.* New York, W. W. Norton, 1958.

DEBOLD, RICHARD C., *LSD, Man and Society.* Middletown, Conn., Wesleyan University Press, 1967.

DEROPP, S., *Drugs and the Mind.* New York, St. Martin's Press, 1957.

EBIN, DAVID, ed., *The Drug Experience.* New York, Grove Press, 1961.

ELDRIDGE, W. B., *Narcotics and the Law.* New York, New York University Press, 1962.

FIDDLE, SEYMOUR, *Portraits from a Shooting Gallery.* New York, Harper & Row, 1967.

FURNAS, J. C., *Life and Times of the Late Demon Rum.* New York, G. P. Putnam's Sons, 1965.

GELLER, ALLEN, and BOAS, MAXWELL, *The Drug Beat.* New York, McGraw-Hill, 1969.

GOODMAN, LOUIS S., and GILMAN, E. Z., eds., *The Pharmacological Basis of Therapeutics.* New York, Macmillan Company, 1965.

GOLDSTEIN, RICHARD, *One in Seven: Drugs on Campus.* New York, Walker & Co., 1966.

HARMS, E., *Drug Addiction in Youth.* New York, Pergamon Press, 1965.

HENTOFF, NAT, *A Doctor Among the Addicts.* New York, Rand McNally and Co., 1968.

HUXLEY, ALDOUS, *The Doors of Perception.* New York, Harper & Row, 1954.

HYDE, MARGARET, *Mind Drugs.* Hightstown, N.J., McGraw-Hill, 1968.

JAFFEE, SAUL, *Narcotics—An American Plan.* New York, Paul S. Eriksson, Inc., 1966.

JONES, HOWARD, *Alcohol Addiction.* London, Tavistock Publications, 1963.

KREIG, MARGARET, *Black Market Medicine.* Englewood Cliffs, N.J., Prentice-Hall, Inc., 1967.

KING, ALEXANDER, *Mine Enemy Grows Older.* New York, Simon & Schuster, 1958.

KRON, YVES J., and BROWN, EDWARD M., *Mainline to Nowhere: The Making of a Heroin Addict.* New York, Pantheon Books, 1965.

LEWIN, LOUIS, *Phantastica, Narcotics and Stimulating Drugs, Their Use and Abuse.* New York, E. P. Dutton & Co., 1964.

LINGEMAN, RICHARD R., *Drugs from A to Z: A Dictionary.* New York, McGraw-Hill, 1969.

LOURIA, DONALD B., MD, *The Drug Scene.* New York, McGraw-Hill, 1968.

MOJCIECHOWSKA, MAIA A., *Tuned Out.* New York, Harper & Row, 1967.

BIBLIOGRAPHY

MASTERS, R. C. L., and HOUSTON, JEAN, *The Varieties of Psychedelic Experience.* New York, Holt, Winston & Rinehart, 1967.

MINTZ, MORTON, *By Prescription Only.* Boston, Houghton, Mifflin Co., 1967.

NOWLIS, HELEN H., *Drugs on the College Campus.* New York, Doubleday & Co., 1969.

O'DONNELL, JOHN A., and BALL, JOHN C., eds., *Narcotic Addiction.* New York, Harper & Row, 1966.

OURSLER, WILL, *Marijuana, the Facts, the Truth.* New York, Paul S. Eriksson, Inc., 1968.

PROGER, SAMUEL, MD, *The Medicated Society.* New York, Macmillan Co., 1968.

RATHBONE, JOSEPHINE L., *Tobacco, Alcohol and Narcotics.* New York, Oxford Book Co., 1952.

SCHULTES, RICHARD E., "Botanical Sources of the New World Narcotics," *Psychedelic Review,* No. 2 (1964).

SLOTKIN, J. S., *The Peyote Religion.* Glencoe, Ill., The Free Press, 1956.

SOLOMON, DAVID, ed., *LSD: The Consciousness Expanding Drug.* New York, G. P. Putnam's Sons, 1964.

————, *The Marihuana Papers.* New York, New American Library, 1966.

STEARNS, J., *The Seekers.* New York, Doubleday & Co., 1961.

SURFACE, WILLIAM, *The Poisoned Ivy.* New York, Coward-McCann, Inc., 1968.

TAYLOR, NORMAN, *Narcotics: Nature's Dangerous Gifts.* New York, Dell Publishing Co., 1966.

Time, editors, *The Drug Takers.* New York, Time Inc. Publishing Co., 1965.

TRICE, HARRISON M., *Alcoholism in America.* New York, McGraw-Hill, 1966.

UHR, LEONARD, and MILLER, J. G., *Drugs and Behavior.* New York, John Wiley & Sons, Inc., 1966.

WALLACE, GEORGE B., "The Rehabilitation of the Drug Addict," *Journal of Educational Sociology,* Vol. 4, No. 6 (1931).

WASSON, R. GORDON, *The Drug Takers.* New York, Time-Life Publishing Co., 1965.

WEIL, ANDREW, *The Natural Mind.* Boston, Houghton Mifflin, 1972.

WILNER, DANIEL M., PhD, and KASSEBAUM, GENE, PhD, eds., *Narcotics.* New York, McGraw-Hill, 1965.

INDEX

DATE DUE